Basic Grammar and Usage

Sixth Edition

Penelope Choy
Los Angeles City College

Dorothy Goldbart Clark
California State University, Northridge

THOMSON

HEINLE

Australia Canada Mexico Singapore Spain United Kingdom United States

Basic Grammar and Usage
Sixth Edition
Penelope Choy and Dorothy Goldbart Clark

Publisher: *Earl McPeek*
Acquisitions Editor: *Steve Dalphin*
Market Strategist: *Katrina Byrd*
Project Manager: *Andrea Archer*

Printed in Canada
8 9 10 11 12 13   07 06 05 04 03 02

For more information contact Heinle, 25 Thomson Place, Boston, MA 02210 USA, or you can visit our Internet site at http://www.heinle.com

For permission to use material from this text or product contact us:
Tel   1-800-730-2214
Fax   1-800-730-2215
Web   www.thomsonrights.com

ISBN: 0-1550-7057-6

Library of Congress Catalog Card Number: 2001089598

PREFACE TO THE SIXTH EDITION

This sixth edition of *Basic Grammar and Usage* preserves the format of the earlier five editions. As in the previous editions, this text contains six units, beginning with the unit on subject-verb identification, which forms the foundation for the rest of the book, and continuing with five other units devoted to specific areas of grammar. The units are divided into individual lessons. Each lesson contains clear explanations of specific grammar rules and structures and includes copious examples of each point. Every lesson is followed by two exercises. Exercise A focuses on the material in that particular lesson. Exercise B reviews material covered in earlier lessons in the unit to ensure that students remember material previously studied and are able to see the relationships among the various lessons. For example, in Unit Three, "Identifying and Punctuating the Main Types of Sentences," students learn how to identify, punctuate, and construct compound sentences in Lesson 9. In Lesson 10, they learn how to do the same things with complex sentences. Lesson 11 explains what run-on sentences and comma splices are and, drawing on the students' knowledge of compound and complex sentences, shows them how to correct these errors. Lesson 12 does the same thing for sentence fragments. A review at the end of each unit tests the students' knowledge of the entire sequence of lessons for that unit.

Throughout the exercises, we have tried to go beyond simple fill-in-the-blank and choose-the-correct-answer items and have emphasized error recognition, such as identifying which sentences contain fragments or run-ons and asking students to correct those mistakes. This emphasis reflects our belief that a primary reason for studying grammar and usage is to help students learn to edit their own compositions and to avoid making errors in the future. The "To the Student" preface explains this process in detail.

Additional exercises are provided in the instructor's manual, which is available on adoption of this text. Brief diagnostic tests are included for each unit so that instructors who do not plan to use the entire text can select units for individual students based on their areas of greatest need. Achievement tests, identical in format to the diagnostic tests, measure what the students have learned after completing each unit. We suggest that the diagnostic tests be given at the beginning of the semester and that the achievement tests be used to evaluate what the students have learned over the course of the semester. The instructor's manual also includes detailed unit tests to supplement the unit reviews contained in the text. These tests may be used for either evaluation or for extra practice. The tests are printed on 8.5 by 11 inch pages for convenient reproduction.

Answers to the "A" exercises are included in the text. The instructor's manual contains answers to the "B" exercises, unit reviews, and all the tests in the manual.

In response to requests from many instructors, the sixth edition includes an online writing section, which presents the basics of paragraph organization.

Instructors who are not using a separate rhetoric now have a composition resource readily available for their students. On the other hand, students whose instructors want only a grammar review will avoid having to pay for a combined text.

Although *Basic Grammar and Usage* was originally designed for students whose first language is English, it has been used successfully throughout the years by students learning English as a second language. In addition to being a classroom text, *Basic Grammar and Usage* can also be used in writing labs and for individual study.

Many people have participated in the preparation of this book. We are grateful to the instructors who have provided us with valuable feedback on the previous editions. In addition, we are grateful to the people at Harcourt College Publishers who have helped in the preparation of this edition. We would also like to thank the team at Impressions Book and Journal Services, and Laura Poole, the copyeditor.

Penelope Choy would like to thank her stepson and endlessly patient computer instructor, Joel Rothman, who helped her prepare the manuscript for this edition, and her husband, Gene Rothman, for his patience and good humor during the months she worked on this text.

Dorothy Clark would like to thank her husband, Kevin O'Neill, for his indefatigable support, creative encouragement, and downright genius; her children, Julia and Ben, for their endless patience; and her students, for the lessons they continue to teach her.

It has now been twenty-three years since the first edition of *Basic Grammar and Usage* appeared. We wish to thank the many instructors and the thousands of students who have used our book during this time. Both of us are still teaching composition courses and still encountering students with little or no knowledge of grammar and usage. We know personally the relief these students feel when they realize that English grammar is comprehensible and systematic. As a math major said, "I was always good in math but terrible in English, and I dreaded taking this course. But then I saw that my grammar errors were problems I could solve by applying the rules in the book." We hope that your students have similarly successful experiences.

Preface to
the First Edition

Basic Grammar and Usage was originally written for students in a special admissions program at the University of California, Los Angeles. As part of their participation in the program, the students were enrolled in a composition and grammar course designed to prepare them for the university's freshman English courses. When the program began in 1971, none of the grammar textbooks then on the market seemed suitable for the students, whose previous exposure to grammar had been cursory or, in some cases, nonexistent. As the director of the program's English classes, I decided to write a book of my own that would cover the most important areas of grammar and usage in a way that would be easily understood by my students.

The original version of *Basic Grammar and Usage* received an enthusiastic response from the students and was used successfully throughout the three-year duration of the program. After the program ended in 1974, many of the instructors asked permission to reproduce the book for use in their new teaching positions. By the time copies of *Basic Grammar and Usage* reached Harcourt Brace Jovanovich in 1975, the text had already been used by more than 1,500 students in nearly a dozen schools.

Basic Grammar and Usage presents material in small segments so that students can master a particular topic one step at a time. The lessons within each unit are cumulative. For example, students doing the pronoun exercises for Lesson 19 will find that those exercises include a review of the constructions treated in Lessons 16 to 18. This approach reinforces the students' grasp of the material and helps them develop the skills they need for the writing of compositions. To make them more interesting to students, the exercises in four of the six units are presented as short narratives rather than as lists of unrelated sentences. Each lesson concludes with two exercises, which may be either used in class or assigned as homework. In addition, each unit ends with a composition that the students must proofread for errors and then correct to demonstrate mastery of the material.

Students who have never before studied grammar systematically will find that working through the text from beginning to end provides an insight into the basic patterns of English grammar. As one student commented on an end-of-course evaluation, "The most important thing I learned from *Basic Grammar and Usage* is that if you learn what an independent clause is, half of your grammar problems are over." On the other hand, students who do not need a total review of grammar can concentrate on the specific areas in which they have weaknesses. To help the instructor evaluate both types of student, the Instructor's Manual accompanying the text includes a diagnostic test and a post-test divided into sections corresponding to the units in the book. There are also separate achievement tests for each unit, as well as answer keys to the exercises presented in the text.

Although *Basic Grammar and Usage* is designed for students whose native language is English, it has been used successfully by students learning English as a second language. In addition to being a classroom text, *Basic Grammar and Usage* can be used in writing labs and for individual tutoring.

Many people have shared in the preparation of *Basic Grammar and Usage*. I wish in particular to thank the instructors and administrators of UCLA's Academic Advancement Program, where this book originated. In revising the text for publication, I have been greatly helped by the suggestions of Regina Sackmary of Queensborough Community College of the City University of New York and by Elizabeth Gavin, formerly of California State University, Long Beach, who reviewed the manuscript for me. Sue Houchins of the Black Studies Center of the Claremont Colleges contributed many ideas and reference materials for the exercises. An author could not ask for more supportive people to work with than the staff of Harcourt Brace Jovanovich. I owe a special debt of gratitude to Raoul Savoie, who first brought the UCLA version of the text to the attention of his company. I also wish to thank Lauren Procton, who was responsible for the editing, and Eben W. Ludlow, who has provided guidance and encouragement throughout all the stages of this book's development.

Penelope Choy

To the Student: Using This Book to Edit Your Compositions

Basic Grammar and Usage is designed to help you master the most important rules of grammar, usage, and grammatical structures. However, learning grammar and usage is only a means to an end, not an end in itself. Learning grammar and usage should ultimately enable you to write better compositions—compositions with clearly written and easily understood sentences that are free of distracting errors that draw your reader's attention away from the important points you are trying to make.

When you write a composition, the first draft of your paper may not be free of grammar and usage errors. However, you can learn to edit your papers; that is, to remove mistakes before you complete the final draft. The first step in this process is for you to know the kinds of mistakes you most often make. Your instructor may give you a pretest to point out areas of grammar and usage that you need to study. You should also keep track of the mistakes you make in your compositions. Then, as you study the lessons, *Basic Grammar and Usage* will explain how to avoid these errors. You can then look for these particular mistakes on the rough drafts of your essays.

The chart displayed on the inside back cover will help you keep track of the kinds of mistakes you make. Notice that there are columns in which you may enter the number and kind of mistakes you make on your papers. There is also a list of corresponding lessons in *Basic Grammar and Usage* in which each mistake is discussed.

Editing your papers will be easier if you prepare your manuscript for proofreading in advance. Whether you are using a typewriter or a word processor, you should triple-space between lines to provide plenty of room to make corrections. If you are writing by hand, write on every other line, and do not write on the back of the page. If you use a word processing software program, it will help to use a large font for your rough draft, to make it easier to read. With a word processor, it is easy to look at one section of a paper at a time. If you are writing by hand, consider writing each paragraph on separate sheets of paper. This way, correcting one paragraph of your essay at a time will not only seem less overwhelming, but it will be easier to completely rewrite a paragraph should you decide it is needed. You will also not have to recopy other parts of the essay.

The authors of *Basic Grammar and Usage* collected the following suggestions (from other English instructors and their best students) to demonstrate how best to edit a paper for grammar and usage errors:

1. Do not try to edit your paper immediately after you finish writing it. Let some time pass so that you do not overlook mistakes because of your familiarity with the paper.

2. Look for one type of error at a time. Try not to proofread for everything at once. For example, if you know that you often write comma splices, check first for that mistake before looking for others.

3. Begin by looking for the mistakes you and/or your instructor consider to be the most serious.

4. Consider reading the paper aloud or recording it into a tape player and listening to it. Read slowly and carefully. If you have any trouble reading the sentences or words, it is a sign that they may be awkwardly written or that they may contain major grammatical errors needing to be corrected.

5. Try reading the paper backwards, from the last sentence to the first. This will help overcome the common problem of overlooking mistakes because of concentrating on the flow of ideas rather than on the mechanics of the grammar and usage. When you read from the back to the front, the sentences will no longer have a familiar continuity. This will make it easier for you to look at each sentence individually and spot mistakes each sentence may contain.

6. On your last reading, move a ruler down the page as you read from beginning to end. This will help you read more slowly and concentrate better on each sentence.

7. Plan on reading your paper several times: one time for each major kind of error and one time for each major revision of your draft.

8. Plan on spending the time necessary for editing your paper properly. This will include time for taking a break between the time you finish the paper and the time you begin editing it, time for proofreading more than once, and time for a final reading of your last draft.

CONTENTS

Unit 6
Capitalization, More Punctuation, Placement of Modifiers, Parallel Structure, and Irregular Verbs 193

U N 1 I T

IDENTIFYING SUBJECTS AND VERBS

SENTENCES WITH ONE SUBJECT AND ONE VERB

The most important grammatical skill you can learn is how to identify subjects and verbs. Just as solving arithmetic problems requires that you know the multiplication tables perfectly, solving grammatical problems requires you to identify subjects and verbs with perfect accuracy. This is not as difficult as it may sound. With practice, recognizing subjects and verbs will become as automatic as knowing that $2 + 2 = 4$.

Although in conversation people often speak in short word groups that may not be complete sentences, in written English people usually use complete sentences.

A complete sentence contains at least one subject and one verb.

A sentence can be thought of as a statement describing an *actor* performing a particular *action*. For example, in the sentence "The dog ran," the *actor* or person performing the action is the dog. What *action* did the dog perform? He *ran*. This

Harcourt, Inc.

actor-action pattern can be found in most sentences. Can you identify the actor and the action in each of the following sentences?

The teacher laughed.

The crowd applauded.

The actor in a sentence is called the **subject.** The action word in a sentence is called the **verb.** Together, the subject and verb form the core of the sentence. Notice that even if extra words are added to the two sentences above, the subject-verb core in each sentence remains the same.

The teacher laughed at the student's joke.

After the performance, the crowd applauded enthusiastically.

You can see that to identify subjects and verbs, you must be able to separate these core words from the rest of the words in the sentence.

Here are some suggestions to help you identify verbs.

1. The *action* words in sentences are verbs. For example,

The team *played* well.

This store *sells* rare books.

The doctor *recommended* vitamins.

Underline the verb in each of the following sentences.

The bank lends money to small businesses.

Gina speaks Italian.

The flood destroyed many homes.

2. All forms of the verb "to be" are verbs: *am, is, are, was, were, and been.* For example,

Susan *is* unhappy.

The actor *was* nervous.

Verbs also include words that can be used as substitutes for forms of *be,* such as *seem, feel, become,* and *appear.* These verbs are called **linking** or **auxiliary verbs.**

Susan *seems* unhappy.

The actor *appeared* nervous.

Underline the verb in each of the following sentences.

Harcourt, Inc.

The children became excited during the birthday party.

The professor seemed fatigued today.

The actors felt happy with their performance.

3. Verbs are the only words that change their spelling to show tense. **Tense** is the time—present, past, or future—at which the verb's action occurs. For example, the sentence "We *walk* each morning" has a present-tense verb. The sentence "We *walked* each morning" has a past-tense verb. Underline the verb in each of the following sentences.

Grandfather moves today.

My brother moved to Chicago last month.

Sandra dances very well.

Maria danced on her wedding day.

I wash my hair every morning.

The nurse washed her hands.

Identifying verbs will be easier for you if you remember that the following kinds of words are *not* verbs.

4. An **infinitive**—the combination of the word *to* plus a verb, such as *to walk* or *to study*—is not considered part of the verb in a sentence. Read the following sentences.

He plans to swim later.

She wants to enter graduate school.

The main verbs in these two sentences are *plans* and *wants*. The infinitives *to swim* and *to enter* are not included. Underline the main verb in each of the following sentences.

Benjy decided to play his new video games.

The conductor promised to check our luggage.

5. **Adverbs**—words that describe a verb—are *not* part of the verb. Many commonly used adverbs end in *-ly*. The adverbs in the following sentences are italicized. Underline the verb in each sentence.

The guitarist played *badly*.

Phillipe rushed *quickly* to our rescue.

The mother *patiently* helped her children.

Harcourt, Inc.

The words *not, never,* and *very* are also adverbs. Like other adverbs, these words are *not* part of the verb. Underline the verb in each of the following sentences. Do *not* include adverbs.

The dancers are not here yet.

He never studies late.

The director spoke very carefully.

He is not a good mechanic.

José never remembers to close the door.

Now that you can identify verbs, here are some suggestions to help you identify subjects.

1. The subject of a sentence is most often a noun. A **noun** is the name of a person, place, or thing, such as *Julia, Houston,* or *pens.* A noun may also be the name of an abstract idea, such as *sadness* or *failure.* Underline the subject in each of the following sentences *once* and the verb *twice.* Remember that the verb is the *action,* and the subject is the *actor.*

   Kevin reads many books each month.

   The store closes at midnight.

   Atlanta hosted the 1996 Olympics.

   Love conquers all.

2. The subject of a sentence may also be a **subject pronoun.** A **pronoun** is a word used in place of a noun, such as *she* (*=Julia*), *it* (*= Houston*), or *they* (*= pens*). The following words are subject pronouns:

   I, you, he, she, it, we, they

   Underline the subject in each of the following sentences *once* and the verb *twice.*

   He was elected president of the United States.

   Each spring they travel to Yosemite National Park.

   I always drink strong coffee.

   We rarely have dinner out on weekdays.

   You washed the dishes last night.

3. The subject of a sentence may also be a **gerund.** A **gerund** is an *-ing* form of a verb used as a noun. For example, in the sentence "Swimming is an excellent form of exercise," the subject of the sentence is the gerund *swimming.* Underline the gerund subjects in the following sentences *once* and the verbs *twice.*

Listening is difficult for young children.

Dieting makes me very hungry.

4. In **commands** (also known as **imperatives**), such as "Wash the dishes!," the subject is understood to be the subject pronoun *you* even though the word *you* is almost never included in the command. *You* is understood to be the subject of the following sentences.

Do your homework early.

Consider the alternative.

Underline the subject in each of the following sentences *once* and the verb *twice*. If the sentence is a command, write the subject *you* in parentheses at the beginning of the sentence.

Remember to wipe your feet before entering.

The judge reviewed the verdict.

They bowl every Wednesday.

Discuss these issues with your colleagues.

Identifying subjects will be easier for you if you remember that the following kinds of words are *not* subjects.

5. **Adjectives**—words that describe a noun—are *not* part of the subject. For example, in the sentence "The tall boy runs well," the subject is "boy," *not* "tall boy." In the sentence "A new car is a great joy," the subject is "car," *not* "new car." Underline the subject in each of the following sentences *once* and the verb *twice*.

A talented singer performed that song.

Chocolate cake is his favorite food.

Small pets delight our family.

An angry, bitter debate ended the program.

6. Words that show **possession,** or ownership, are *not* part of the subject. Words that show possession include nouns ending in an apostrophe (') combined with *s,* such as *Dina's* or *cat's.* They also include **possessive pronouns,** words that replace nouns showing ownership, such as *hers* (= *Dina's*) or *its* (= *cat's*). Possessive pronouns include the following words:

my, your, his, hers, its, our, their

Because words that show possession are *not* part of the subject, in the sentence "My dog has fleas," the subject is "dog," *not* "my dog." In the sentence "Sarah's mother is a doctor," the subject is "mother," *not* "Sarah's mother." Underline the subject in each of the following sentences *once* and the verb *twice*.

His daughter became a doctor.

My brother works in another city.

This beach's beauty is startling.

Harry's car needs a new battery.

Here is a final suggestion to help you identify subjects and verbs accurately.

Try to identify the verb in a sentence before you try to identify the subject.

A sentence may have many nouns, any of which could be the subject, but it will usually have only one or two verbs. For example,

The director of the play shouted angry words to all the actors and staff.

There are five nouns in the above sentence (*director, play, words, actors, staff*), any of which might be the subject. However, there is only one verb—*shouted.* Once you have identified the verb as *shouted,* all you have to ask yourself is "Who or what shouted?" The answer is *director,* which is the subject of the sentence.

Identify the subject and verb in the following sentence, remembering to look for the verb first.

In the winter, our family travels to the mountains for our vacation.

Remember these basic points:

1. The action being performed in a sentence is the **verb.**
2. The person or thing performing the action is the **subject.**
3. A sentence consists of an *actor* performing an *action,* or, in other words, a **subject** plus a **verb.**

Every sentence you write will have a subject and a verb, so you must be able to identify subjects and verbs to write correctly. Therefore, as you do the exercises in this unit, apply the rules you have learned in each lesson, and think about what you are doing. Do not make random guesses. Grammar is based on logic, not on luck.

Underline the subject in each of the following sentences *once* and the verb *twice*. Add the subject *you* in parentheses if the sentence is a command.

Harcourt, Inc.

That man won the contest yesterday.

Success makes us happy.

The ancient horse slowly pulled the cart.

Wisdom is endless.

Consider the virtues of discipline.

My little sister's dance recital was lots of fun.

A quiet garden is my favorite place to read.

Your family's last vacation sounds very exciting.

EXERCISE
1A

Underline the subject of each sentence *once* and each verb *twice*. Each sentence has only one subject and one verb. *Remember to look for the verb first* before you try to find the subject.

1. Many Americans now invest in the stock market.

2. In the past, most stock market investors were already wealthy.

3. Today, 401(k) plans allow ordinary workers to invest part of their salary in the stock market.

4. Employees use these plans to save for retirement or to buy new homes.

5. Mutual funds also help people to invest smaller amounts of money.

6. Some funds accept purchases of as little as $50 at a time.

7. In the past, investors had to use stockbrokers to buy stocks and bonds for them.

8. Now, they purchase securities at home by phone or on their personal computers.

9. Professional stockbrokers used to be the main source of financial information.

10. Now, financial programs appear on cable television all day long.

11. Investors also surf the World Wide Web to find the latest economic news.

12. They read financial magazines like *Money, Mutual Funds,* and *Business Week.*

13. Casual conversations often focus on the stock market.

14. Any social gathering gives people a chance to compare their investment portfolios.

15. Personal advice columns even tell lonely singles to enroll in investment classes to meet potential mates.

16. Wise investments help people to plan for a secure future.

17. However, losing money in the stock market is always possible.

18. Like any other financial venture, investing in the stock market requires good information and careful planning.

Harcourt, Inc.

EXERCISE
1B

Underline the subject of each sentence *once* and the verb *twice*. Each sentence has one subject and one verb. *Remember to look for the verb first* before you try to locate the subject.

1. Today, many people worry about endangered animals.

2. Hawaiian monk seals are an example.

3. The seals live in Hawaii's coral reefs.

4. They depend on the reefs for protection from natural enemies, such as sharks.

5. However, human activity endangers these reefs.

6. The fishing industry creates most of the problems.

7. Their boats' trash washes onto the reefs.

8. Old fishing nets present the most danger.

9. The nets trap the seals in their folds.

10. Many seals fail to escape from the nets.

11. They then die a slow death from drowning.

12. Other nets break off huge chunks of the reef.

13. Over time, these actions destroy portions of the reef.

14. Protecting the reefs and the seals is important to conservationists.

15. Volunteers patrol the reefs to look for animals in danger.

16. Divers work to collect tons of debris from the reefs.

17. The debris includes marine lines, old batteries, and plastic containers, as well as the fishing nets.

18. Low-flying planes help to locate areas for the volunteers to clean.

19. Removing the trash protects both the reefs and the monk seals.

20. Hawaii's efforts to save endangered animals provide an example for conservationists everywhere.

Harcourt, Inc.

C H A 2 P T E R

Multiple Subjects and Verbs

Some sentences have more than one subject. Others have more than one verb. Many sentences have more than one subject *and* more than one verb. The subjects in the following sentences have been labeled with an "S" and the verbs with a "V."

   S V   V
He swam and fished this summer.

       S   S   V
The dog and kitten became good friends.

   S V   S   V
She danced well, and the director applauded.

     S V   S   V
When we study hard, we usually do well.

Harcourt, Inc.

You can identify the pattern of a sentence by indicating how many subjects and verbs it has. In theory a sentence can have any number of subjects and verbs, but these are the most common patterns:

S-V   one subject and one verb

S-V-V   one subject and two verbs

S-S-V   two subjects and one verb

S-V/S-V   two subjects and two verbs

Underline the subjects of the following sentences *once* and the verbs *twice*.

The parrot squawked loudly.

His job started early and ended quite late.

Gardening and decorating were Beatrice's joys.

The team won the game, but the captain was not happy.

Any group of words that contains *at least one subject and one verb* is called a **clause**. A single sentence may have one clause or more than one clause.

S-V   one clause   The boy ate his pizza slice.

S-V-V   one clause   Sonya danced and sang.

S-S-V   one clause   The judge and jury joked.

S-V/S-V   two clauses   The dog barked, / and we laughed.

S-V-V/S-V two clauses   He hiked and fished / when the sun rose.

Later in this book we will study the different types of clauses to understand how they determine punctuation. For now, the important thing is to learn to find all the subjects and verbs in each sentence.

Something to keep in mind when looking for multiple subjects and verbs is that the *length* of the sentence won't necessarily tell you whether the sentence has one clause or several clauses. Look at these two sentences:

She sang, but I danced. (How many clauses?)

The anxious, nervous young bride tripped on the stairs. (How many clauses?)

The first sentence is short—only five words—but it has two S-V patterns and, therefore, two clauses (*she sang,* but *I danced*). The second sentence is more than twice as long as the first, but it has only one clause (*bride . . . tripped*). So don't be fooled by the length of the sentence: Some short sentences have multiple subjects and verbs, and some long sentences have only a single clause (S-V).

Harcourt, Inc.

The sentences below are skeleton sentences. That is, they are stripped down to only subjects, verbs, and connecting words. Go through them, underlining the subjects *once* and the verbs *twice*.

Sarah laughed and joked.

Julia and Ben argued and fought.

The poet, the artist, and the teacher spoke.

After the game ended, we had lunch.

Laughter invigorates, and love binds.

Because it snowed, we stayed home.

When the movie ended, we left.

The philosopher and his ideas were exciting.

As we watched and waited, the river flooded.

If you go, I stay.

Janice wrote and slept.

As we listened, the storyteller entranced us.

He cried while she packed.

Watch your spelling!   (Did you remember to put *You* in front?)

The practice sentences below have multiple subjects and verbs, but they also include the other types of words you studied in Chapter 1. Before you try them, review that chapter quickly to remind yourself about **adverbs** and **infinitives**, which are never part of the verb, and about **adjectives** and **possessives**, which are not part of the subject. Underline verbs *twice* and subjects *once*.

My uncles and aunts contribute to our family.

The long road seemed to run on for miles and miles.

Duane, José, and Clarence always loved to play soccer.

The gymnastic tournament finally ended, and the players went home.

After the spring semester ended, we partied a lot.

The terribly boring professor lectured monotonously to his class of students.

The boy's mother and father decided to send him to space camp.

The jury's verdict gladdened and relieved us.

The story's ending surprised us, but we still liked it.

Our new, fancy, expensive car has a CD player and a sun roof.

Keep off the grass, and don't pick the flowers!

Harcourt, Inc.

EXERCISE
2A

Underline the subjects of the following sentences *once* and the verbs *twice*. To help you, the pattern of each sentence is indicated in parentheses.

1. If you are in Oklahoma City, try to visit the National Cowboy and Western Heritage Museum. (S-V/S-V)

2. The museum occupies 220,000 square feet and has a collection of more than 19,000 objects. (S-V-V)

3. The museum contains many separate galleries, and each gallery features a different aspect of Western life. (S-V/S-V)

4. The Native American Gallery honors this country's original inhabitants and contains a wide variety of Indian artifacts. (S-V-V)

5. Beadwork, pottery, basketry, and carvings represent the heritage of various Native American tribes. (S-S-S-S-V)

6. The museum's former name was the National Cowboy Hall of Fame, and a large gallery pays tribute to America's cowboys. (S-V/S-V)

7. Barbed wire enabled ranchers to raise cattle on the prairies, and this gallery has one of the world's largest barbed wire collections. (S-V/S-V)

8. Mexican American cowboys played important roles in the West, and the gallery's collections include their distinctive costumes and equipment. (S-V/S-V)

9. Rodeos provided entertainment in the West, and another gallery re-creates a 1950s rodeo arena. (S-V/S-V)

10. Visitors view interactive exhibits of the main rodeo events and learn about calf roping, bull riding, and steer wrestling. (S-V-V)

11. Most Americans learned about the West from movies and television, and the Western Entertainment Gallery commemorates cowboy actors like Gene Autry and Hopalong Cassidy and television shows like *Bonanza* and *The Big Valley*. (S-V/S-V)

12. Prosperity Junction re-creates life in a turn-of-the-century cattle town. (S-V)

13. Museum guests explore the life-size buildings and visit the town's schoolhouse, church, saloon, and doctor's office. (S-V-V)

14. A special Children's Cowboy Corral allows children to play inside a teepee and a pioneer's covered wagon. (S-V)

15. The museum's art galleries display nineteenth- and twentieth-century Western paintings and sculptures. (S-V)

16. The museum is a fascinating place to visit, and it gives its guests valuable information about an important period in American history. (S-V/S-V)

EXERCISE
2B

Underline the subjects of the following sentences *once* and the verbs *twice*. Some sentences have more than one subject, more than one verb, or both.

1. Although few people really understand technological advancements, these scientific advancements truly affect our lives.

2. Biotechnology excites some people, but scares others.

3. Although biotechnology has many uses, it especially helps farmers.

4. Few city people worry about soil, but conserving topsoil is important to farmers.

5. Biotechnology helps farmers because its new crops require less disturbance of the soil.

6. This new science gives farmers choices, for they learn new ways to grow their crops.

7. Some people like this research because it also eliminates pesticide use for certain crops.

8. For some hopeful scientists, this research provides an answer to world starvation.

9. Because biotechnology inspires the creation of new, more nutritious foods, these scientists see a future without hunger.

10. However, many people worry about the effects of this new science, and they voice their concerns loudly.

11. Although these people admire scientific advances, they fear them, too.

12. According to these people, such advances interfere with nature's plan.

13. If cotton's molecular structure changes, nobody really gets hurt.

14. However, if edible plants have new molecular structures, those changes pose a potential danger, in these critics' opinion.

15. Perhaps a technologically altered tomato is a new, possibly dangerous, species.

16. These new creations, then, pose possible health dangers because we still need more research about them.

17. Critics emphasize the possible negative effects of biotechnology.

18. For example, it is possible for some new plants to hurt beneficial insects as well as harmful ones.

19. Yet these criticisms sound exaggerated to supporters of biotechnology because its possible benefits seem so wonderful.

20. Though both sides present strong arguments, time is the true test of this new technology.

21. Meanwhile, we eat new foods and hope for the best.

CHAPTER 3

DISTINGUISHING BETWEEN OBJECTS OF PREPOSITIONS AND SUBJECTS

One of the most common causes of errors in identifying the subject of a sentence is confusing it with a noun used as the object of a preposition. This kind of error can also lead to mistakes in subject-verb agreement. (Subject-verb agreement is covered in Unit Two of this book.) To avoid making this type of mistake, you first must learn to recognize prepositions and prepositional phrases.

Prepositions are the short words in our language that show the *position* or relationship between one word and another. For example, if you were trying to describe where a particular store was located, you might say:

The store is *on* the right.

The store is *near* the highway.

The store is *by* the bank.

The store is *under* the elm tree.

The store is *behind* the garage.

Harcourt, Inc.

The italicized words are all prepositions. They indicate the position of the store in relation to the right, the freeway, the bank, the elm tree, and the garage.

Here is a list of the most common prepositions. You do not have to memorize these words, but you must be able to recognize them as prepositions when you see them.

about	between	of
above	beyond	on
across	by	onto
after	concerning	out
against	down	over
along	during	through
amid	except	to
among	for	toward
around	from	under
at	in	up
before	inside	upon
behind	into	with
below	like	within
beneath	near	without
beside		

As you can see from the example sentences describing the location of the store, prepositions are not used by themselves; they are always placed in front of a noun or pronoun. The noun or pronoun following the preposition is called the **object of the preposition.** The group of words containing the preposition and its object is called a **prepositional phrase.** Any words, such as adjectives or the words *a, an,* or *the,* that come between the preposition and its object are also part of the prepositional phrase. Read the following sentences, in which the prepositional phrases are italicized. Notice that each prepositional phrase begins with a preposition and ends with a noun or pronoun.

I leaned *against the car.*

He walked *toward the nearest exit.*

The glass *of orange juice* costs fifty cents.

She stood *beside me.*

Some prepositional phrases may have more than one object.

Harcourt, Inc.

You may sit *near Jane or Susan.*

You may have some *of the bread or waffles.*

It is also possible to have two or more prepositional phrases in a row.

We looked *for the clues in the forest.*

The director *of that movie at the local theater* is sitting by us.

Circle the prepositional phrases in the following sentences. Some sentences may have more than one prepositional phrase.

The policeman looked carefully around the room.

The keys to the car are in the glove compartment.

I gave your recipe to my next-door neighbor.

Ruth came to the party with me.

Construct sentences of your own containing prepositional phrases. Use the prepositions listed below. Make certain that each of your sentences contains at least one subject and one verb.

with: _____

through: _____

by: _____

of: _____

at: _____

The words *before* and *after* may be used either as prepositions or as conjunctions (see below). If the word is being used as a preposition, it will be followed by a noun or pronoun object. If the word is being used as a conjunction, it will be followed by both a subject and a verb.

As a Preposition	**As a Conjunction**
I go to bed *before midnight.*	*Before* you leave the house, be sure to lock the door.
Bob entered the room *after me.*	*After* the bell rang, the students left the room.

Harcourt, Inc.

What do prepositional phrases have to do with identifying subjects and verbs? The answer is simple.

Any word that is part of a prepositional phrase cannot be the subject or the verb of a sentence.

This rule works for two reasons:

1. Any noun or pronoun in a prepositional phrase must be the object of the preposition, and the object of a preposition cannot also be a subject.
2. Prepositional phrases never contain verbs.

To see how this rule can help you identify subjects and verbs, read the following seventeen-word sentence:

At the height of the rush hour, my car stalled in the middle of a busy intersection.

If you want to find the subject and verb of this sentence, you know that they will not be part of any of the sentence's prepositional phrases. So, cross out all the prepositional phrases in the sentence.

~~At the height of the rush hour,~~ my car stalled ~~in the middle of a busy intersection.~~

You now have only three words left out of the original seventeen, and you know that the subject and verb must be within these three words. What are the subject and verb?

Read the following sentence, and cross out all of its prepositional phrases.

In the evening she works on her assignments for the next day.

If you crossed out all the prepositional phrases, you should be left with only two words—the subject *she* and the verb *works*.

Identify the subject and verb in the following sentence. Cross out the prepositional phrases first.

On the way to their hotel, a group of tourists stopped at a souvenir shop.

If you have identified all of the prepositional phrases, you should be left with only three words—*a group* and *stopped*. Which word is the subject, and which is the verb?

Harcourt, Inc.

Now you can see another reason why it is important to be able to identify prepositional phrases. It might seem logical for the subject of the sentence to be *tourists*. However, because *of tourists* is a prepositional phrase, *tourists* cannot be the subject. Instead, the subject is *group*.

What is the subject of the following sentence?

Many members of Congress are lawyers.

If you crossed out the prepositional phrase *of Congress*, you would know that the subject is *members*, not *Congress*.

Underline the subjects of the following sentences *once* and the verbs *twice*. Remember to cross out the prepositional phrases first.

During the oil shortage, the price of gas increased.

The car with the dented fender belongs to Carolyn.

A house in Beverly Hills with three bedrooms and two bathrooms sells for over $800,000.

The stores in the mall open at ten in the morning.

The driver of the red Corvette skidded into the center lane.

One of the employees received a $50 raise.

Your clothes from the dry cleaner are in the closet.

EXERCISE
3A

Underline the subjects of the following sentences *once* and the verbs *twice*. Some sentences may have more than one subject, more than one verb, or both. Remember to cross out the prepositional phrases first.

1. One of the legendary figures of American history is Sacajawea.

2. With her French fur trapper husband, Sacajawea served as a guide for the famous Lewis and Clark expedition of 1805–1806.

3. The purpose of this expedition was to explore the lands between St. Louis, Missouri, and the Pacific Ocean.

4. With her many talents, Sacajawea helped to make the expedition a success.

5. In her role as an interpreter, Sacajawea communicated with many Native American tribes along the expedition's route.

6. Her knowledge of edible plants enabled the group to avoid starvation during their two-year trip.

7. In addition, the presence of a woman in the expedition assured the Native Americans of the group's peaceful intent.

8. According to William Clark, "A woman with a party of men is a token of peace."

9. With Sacajawea's ability to gain information from local tribes about routes through the mountains, the expedition made its way successfully across the continent.

10. The explorers traveled up the Missouri River, across the Rockies, and down the Snake and Columbia Rivers to finally reach the Pacific Ocean.

11. The history of Sacajawea's life after the end of the expedition is uncertain.

12. In one version of the story, Sacajawea and her husband moved to St. Louis, and she died of a fever in that city in 1812.

13. In another version, she returned to live with her own Shoshoni tribe on the Wind River Reservation in northern Wyoming and died there at an advanced age in 1884.

14. In the year 2000, the government issued a one-dollar gold coin in honor of this brave woman and of her contributions to the exploration of America.

Harcourt, Inc.

EXERCISE
3B

Underline the subjects of the following sentences *once* and the verbs *twice*. Some sentences may have more than one subject, more than one verb, or both. Remember to cross out the prepositional phrases first.

1. Nowadays, many people hear about hypertext, but not everyone understands its use or meaning.

2. In the worlds of computers and cyberspace, the mention of hypertext creates no confusion at all.

3. According to one commentator, "hyper" now means new, nonlinear space.

4. Print text is linear because it requires us to read in a straight line, one word after another, one line after another.

5. Hypertext allows freer movement.

6. Although these ideas about computers seem difficult, they are very understandable.

7. The idea of "links" is at the heart of hypertext , and these "links" allow a reader to connect ideas from many different sources.

8. For example, if a student of baseball seeks information about the sport on her computer, she sees many different "links" from which to choose.

9. On her screen, she sees a "link" to the Baseball Hall of Fame, a link to Mickey Mantle, a link to Hank Aaron, and to other great baseball figures.

10. Our student of baseball and computers reads information about Mickey Mantle, and then she "clicks" to another link about a particular game.

11. Because our baseball student moves from link to link, her choices are open-ended.

12. She is in the new world of hypertext.

13. One commentator of this new concept describes it in an interesting way.

14. At the risk of sounding too casual, this commentator compares hypertext choices to our trips down a supermarket aisle.

15. If you think about the cereal aisle, for example, and about all of the different kinds of cereals, you have an idea about our many opportunities for choice.

16. In a very real way, the World Wide Web's links give us the same type of choices.

17. The world of hypertext is also like an Advent calendar because the text continuously gives us new windows to open.

18. With printed text, the author of the work determines the order of the sentences, paragraphs, pages, and chapters.

19. The physical structure of the printed book also determines the order of its material, and this order of printed books confines us to the physical dimensions of length, breadth, and width.

20. In contrast, the world of digital and electronic text is without these limits.

21. With hypertext, an idea includes a multidimensional network of pointers to whole new groups of ideas, so ideas exist at many levels.

22. One user of this new medium describes it as a collection of elastic messages because the reader of these messages has the power to shrink or to stretch them.

23. Once a student of any subject learns about the possibilities of hypertext, the digital world becomes almost hypnotic in its attraction.

24. Without a doubt, the existence of hypertext changes our way of reading and learning.

MAIN VERBS AND HELPING VERBS

Verbs can be either **main verbs** or **helping** (also called **auxiliary**) **verbs.** Main verbs are the kind of verb you have already studied. Main verbs tell what action is being performed in a sentence. For example,

I *drive* to work each day.

This restaurant *serves* Mexican food.

Helping verbs are used in combination with main verbs. They perform two major functions:

1. Helping verbs indicate shades of meaning that cannot be expressed by a main verb alone. Consider the differences in meaning in the following sentences, in which the helping verbs have been italicized.

I *may* marry you soon.   I *must* marry you soon.

I *should* marry you soon.   I *can* marry you soon.

As you can see, changing the helping verb changes the meaning of the entire sentence. These differences in meaning could not be expressed simply by using the main verb *marry* alone.

2. Helping verbs also show tense—the time at which the action of the verb takes place. Notice how changing the helping verb in the following sentences helps change the tense of the main verb *visit*. (Both the helping verbs and the main verbs have been italicized.)

He *is visiting* New York.

He *will visit* New York.

He *has visited* New York.

Notice the position that helping verbs have in a sentence. They always *come before* the main verb, although sometimes another word, such as an adverb, may come between the helping verb and the main verb.

The team *can win* the game.

The team *can* probably *win* the game.

You *should stay* in bed today.

You *should* definitely *stay* in bed today.

If a question contains a helping verb, the helping verb still *comes before* the main verb.

Can the team *win* the game?

Should you *stay* in bed today?

Does the car *run* well?

When *is* the plane *departing*?

The following words are helping verbs. *Memorize them.*

can, could

may, might, must

shall, should

will, would

The following words can be used either as helping verbs or as main verbs. They are helping verbs if they are used in combination with a main verb. They are main verbs if they occur alone. *Memorize them.*

has, have, had (forms of the verb *have*)

does, do, did, done (forms of the verb *do*)

am, is, are, was, were, been (forms of the verb *be*)

As Main Verbs	**As Helping Verbs**
He *has* my book.	He *has gone* home.
She *did* a headstand.	She *did* not *arrive* on time.
We *are* hungry.	We *are eating* soon.

From now on, whenever you are asked to identify the verbs in a sentence, *include all the main verbs and all the helping verbs.* For example, in the sentence "We should review this lesson," the complete verb is "should review." In the sentence "He has lost his wallet," the verb is "has lost." Underline the complete verbs in the following sentences.

Gail must borrow some money.

I may go to Hawaii this summer.

Sheila can speak German fluently.

We are leaving soon.

Some sentences may contain more than one helping verb.

one helping verb	The mechanic *is working* on your car.
two helping verbs	He *must have lost* your phone number.
three helping verbs	That bill *should have been paid* by now.

Underline the subjects of the following sentences *once* and the complete verbs *twice*.

You could have sold your car for a better price.

The weather will be getting warmer soon.

You have not been listening to me.

Do you have a part-time job?

You should have gone to the dentist last week.

My cousin may be visiting me this summer.

Remember this rule:

The verbs in a sentence include all the main verbs plus all the helping verbs.

Exercise
4A

Underline the subjects of the following sentences *once* and the complete verbs *twice*. Some sentences may have more than one subject, more than one set of verbs, or both. Remember to cross out prepositional phrases first.

1. The moringa tree has been described as "a common tree with rare powers."

2. This tree may provide ways to fight poor nutrition and illness in many parts of the world.

3. Nearly 1 billion people around the world are suffering from malnutrition.

4. Their diets are lacking in important vitamins and minerals.

5. The leaves of the moringa tree contain large amounts of protein, calcium, potassium, iron, and vitamins A and C.

6. The leaves are pulverized, and the powder is used as a dietary supplement.

7. In the African country of Malawi, moringa's vitamin A is preventing childhood blindness.

8. In Senegal, moringa supplements are being given to nursing mothers and their infants.

9. Using moringa will help to prevent many infant deaths from malnutrition.

10. In addition to the nutritional value of the leaves, moringa seeds can be used to purify water supplies.

11. Populations with high rates of malnutrition often also lack sources of clean water.

12. The moringa seeds work better than chemical water purifiers, and they are much cheaper.

13. In medical experiments, skin infections have been treated successfully with an antibiotic from the moringa's seeds and roots.

14. The moringa skin ointments were shown to be as effective as expensive prescription drugs like Neomycin.

15. The seeds of the moringa can also be crushed to provide cooking oil and machinery lubricants.

16. Moringas are found in areas of the world with high rates of malnutrition, disease, and bad water.

17. They can grow in poor soil with little water, and a seed can become a fifteen-foot tree in one year.

18. For all of these reasons, moringas will play an important role in improving living conditions around the world.

Harcourt, Inc.

EXERCISE
4B

Underline the subjects of the following sentences *once* and the complete verbs *twice*. Some sentences may have more than one subject, more than one set of verbs, or both. Remember to cross out prepositional phrases first.

1. Have you been on diets a lot?

2. I have been on diets for a very long time!

3. When I was a child, I must have been very thin.

4. I would eat candy, cakes, and French fries without gaining an ounce!

5. In fact, people would joke about me, and I was embarrassed about my too-thin body.

6. Those times have long gone away!

7. If I even glance at a hot dog, I gain weight!

8. I have tried the all-protein diet, but it made me sick.

9. In that diet, you can have all the protein in the world, but you cannot eat very many carbohydrates, like breads and potatoes.

10. I would have lots of bacon and eggs every morning, and then I would eat hamburger patties without buns for lunch.

11. Dinner would often consist of two steaks with more eggs.

12. Although I must have lost several pounds, I felt hungry and unwell all the time.

13. Have you ever been a vegetarian?

14. Well, I switched from meat and protein to all vegetables and rice.

15. I had eaten a lot of bananas, apples, and pears before I stopped this diet.

16. Hamburgers and hot dogs have always made me very happy.

17. How could I give them up?

18. Now I have found another way to diet, and this way may be the best.

19. I now eat small amounts of any food all day long, and this method has been working for me.

20. This pattern of eating is called "grazing."

21. Unfortunately, I have been using this diet for only two days, and it too may not last!

Harcourt, Inc.

UNIT REVIEW

IDENTIFYING SUBJECTS AND VERBS

Underline the subjects of the following sentences *once* and the complete verbs *twice*. Some sentences may have more than one subject, more than one verb, or both.

1. Modern English is a combination of many languages.

2. During the fifth century A.D., the Anglo-Saxons conquered Britain.

3. These tribes came from northern Europe and spoke a Germanic language.

4. The Germanic language of the Anglo-Saxons forms the basis of English.

5. Most of our common, everyday words are derived from Anglo-Saxon.

6. Examples include words like *mother, father, good, bad, eat,* and *drink.*

7. During the eighth and ninth centuries, Vikings from Scandinavia attacked parts of England.

8. Eventually, the northern half of England was ruled by Viking kings.

9. In this way, Scandinavian words like *sky* and *skin* became part of the English language.

10. Except for Anglo-Saxon, the most important contributor to the English language has been French.

11. French entered the English language when William of Normandy conquered England in 1066 and became its king.

12. Because the Normans now ruled England, the wealthy and important people of the country spoke French.

Harcourt, Inc.

13. The Anglo-Saxons called a woman "pretty"; to the Norman French, she was "beautiful."

14. During the next 400 years, Anglo-Saxon and French blended to form the ancestor of modern English.

15. During the Middle Ages, all university classes were conducted in Latin, and educated people of that time read both Latin and Greek.

16. Even today, many scientific terms in our language have been formed from Greek and Latin roots.

17. For instance, *astronaut* was produced from the Greek words for *star* (*astron*) and *sailor* (*nautilos*).

18. In modern times, American English has also been influenced by other languages.

19. The early American settlers borrowed words like *squash* from the Indians, *rodeo* from the Spanish, and *cookie* from the Dutch.

20. Because so many different languages have contributed words to English, the spelling of English words is sometimes irregular.

21. Some words are spelled like French, and the spelling of other words resembles German, Latin, or Greek.

22. So if you have trouble with spelling, now you know one of the reasons for your problem.

Harcourt, Inc.

U N 2 I T

SUBJECT-VERB AGREEMENT

CHAPTER 5

Recognizing Singular and Plural Subjects and Verbs

Errors in **subject-verb agreement** are among the most common grammatical mistakes. By applying the rules in this unit, you should be able to correct many of the errors in your own writing.

As you already know, a sentence must contain both a subject and a verb. Read the following two sentences. What is the grammatical difference between them?

The bank opens at ten o'clock in the morning.

The banks open at ten o'clock in the morning.

In the first sentence, the subject *bank* is singular. **Singular** means "one." There is *one* bank in the first sentence. In the second sentence, the subject *banks* is plural. **Plural** means "two or more." There are at least two (and possible more than two) banks in the second sentence.

Like the subject *bank*, the verb *opens* in the first sentence is singular. Verb forms ending in *-s* are used with *singular* subjects, as in the sentence "The bank *opens* at ten o'clock in the morning." The verb *open* in the second sentence above is plural. This verb form (without a final *-s*) is used with *plural* subjects, as in the sentence "The banks *open* at ten o'clock in the morning."

In other words, if the subject of a sentence is *singular,* the verb in the sentence must also be *singular.* If the subject of the sentence is *plural,* the verb must be *plural.* This matching of singular subjects with singular verbs and plural subjects with plural verbs is called **subject-verb agreement.**

To avoid making mistakes in subject-verb agreement, you must be able to recognize the difference between singular and plural subjects and verbs.

The subjects of sentences are usually nouns or pronouns. As you know, the plurals of nouns are usually formed by adding an *-s* to singular forms.

Singular	*Plural*
envelope	envelopes
restaurant	restaurants

However, a few nouns (under 1 percent) have irregular plural forms.

Singular	*Plural*
man	men
leaf	leaves
child	children
thesis	theses
self	selves
medium	media (as in the "mass media")

Those pronouns that can be used as subjects are also singular or plural, depending on whether they refer to one or more than one person or thing.

Singular	*Plural*
I	we
you	you
he, she, it	they

Notice that the pronoun *you* may be either singular or plural.

If nouns show number by adding *-s* to the plural, what do verbs do to show whether they are singular or plural? A long time ago English verbs had many different endings for this purpose, but most of those endings have been dropped. Today most English verbs look the same whether the subject is singular or plural: "I talk," "we talk," "the men talk," "I remembered," "they remembered," "the class remembered," and so on. However, there is one place where English verbs have kept a

Harcourt, Inc.

special ending to show number. That special ending is also an *-s*, and the place it is added is in the present-tense singular with the subject pronouns *he, she, it* and with any singular noun that could replace any of these pronouns. Look at these sentences in the present tense, and notice when the *-s* is added to the verb:

Singular	*Plural*
I talk.	We talk.
You talk.	You talk.
He talks.	They talk.
She talks.	They talk.
It talks.	They talk.
The man talks.	The men talk.
The girl talks.	The girls talk.

To sum up, although adding an *-s* to most nouns (99 percent) makes them plural, some singular verbs also end with an *-s*. An easy way to remember this difference is to memorize this rule:

Any verb ending in *-s* is singular.

There are no exceptions to this rule. Therefore, it is not **good usage** in college writing to have a sentence in which a plural subject is matched with a verb ending in *-s*.

Effective writers are as aware of **usage** as they are of grammar. Good usage means choosing different kinds of language for different situations, just as we choose different clothes for different situations. In **informal** situations, such as conversations with friends, it is common to choose informal usage. However, almost all of the writing you do for college is in **formal** situations, such as exams and essay assignments. The difference between formal and informal usage can be seen when we make subjects agree with their verbs. Because most conversation is very informal, you may have heard or have used many informal verb choices in your own conversations. Notice the differences in usage in these examples:

Informal	*Formal*
We was here.	We were here.
He don't come here.	He doesn't come here.
They was at the beach.	They were at the beach.

You want your college writing to be as effective as you can make it. In college you must choose **formal usage** in almost every situation—essays, reports, exams, and so on. The exercises in this book are *always* designed for you to choose formal usage.

To avoid subject-verb agreement errors, there are some rules that you should keep in mind. (How you "keep rules in mind" is up to you. If you find that even after you study rules, you still cannot remember them, you should *memorize* the rules in this unit.)

Rule 1. A verb agrees with the subject, not with the complement. A **complement** is a word that refers to the same person or thing as the subject of the sentence. It follows a linking verb.

S   LV   C
Our main economic *problem is* rising prices.

In the sentence above, the subject is *problem,* which is singular. The subject is not *prices.* Rather, *prices* is the complement. Therefore, the linking verb takes the singular form *is* to agree with *problem.* If the sentence is reversed, it reads:

S   LV   C
Rising *prices are* our main economic problem.

The subject is now the plural noun *prices,* and *problem* is the complement. The verb now takes the plural form *are.* Which are the correct verbs in the following sentences?

The topic of discussion (was, were) political refugees.

Astrological signs (seems, seem) to be an interesting subject to many people.

Rule 2. Prepositional phrases have no effect on a verb.

The *president,* with his chief economic advisors, is having a press conference today.

In the sentence above, the subject is singular (*president*). The prepositional phrase, *with his chief economic advisors,* has no effect on the verb, which remains singular (*is having*).

A hamburger with French fries costs $2.

The singular verb *costs* agrees with the singular subject *hamburger.* The prepositional phrase *with French fries* has no effect on the verb. Which is the correct verb in the following sentence?

The woman with her ten cats (was, were) evicted for breaking the clause in her lease that prohibited the keeping of pets.

Harcourt, Inc.

In addition, do not mistakenly make your verb agree with a noun or pronoun in a prepositional phrase. (This is easy to do because many prepositional phrases come just before a verb.)

The *problems* of this school district *trouble* the school board greatly.

In the sentence above, the subject is plural (*problems*). The plural verb *trouble* agrees with *problems,* not with the singular object of the preposition (*district*).

The attitude of adolescents is often difficult to understand.

The singular verb *is* agrees with the singular subject *attitude,* not with the plural object of the preposition (*adolescents*).

Which are the correct verbs in the following sentences?

One of the restaurants (serves, serve) Thai food.

The directions for the test (was, were) confusing.

Rule 3. Be especially alert for subject-verb agreement when the sentence has **inverted word order,** as in these three situations:

a) **Questions**

Notice the location of the subject in these questions:

    HV S MV
Does he want a new car? (subject between helping and main verb)

    V   S
Is turkey your favorite food? (subject after main verb)

Interrogative words like *when, where,* and *how* come at the beginning of sentence patterns, but they are never subjects.

        HV   S   MV
When *does the game start?* (subject between helping and main verb)

        MV   S
Where *is the picnic?* (subject after verb)

        HV S MV
How *can he study* all weekend? (subject between helping and main verb)

Harcourt, Inc.

b)   Sentence patterns beginning with *here* or *there*

The words *here* and *there* are never subjects.
Notice the location of the subject in these patterns:

There *are* many *children* here today. (subject after verb)

Here *are* your test *results*. (subject after verb)

c)   Rare patterns in which the verb precedes the subject

Occasionally a writer will, for emphasis, put a subject after its verb.
Notice the location of the subject in these sentences:

Behind the lamp in the corner *was* the very expensive statue. (If the order of this sentence were reversed, it would read, "The very expensive statue was behind the lamp in the corner.")

Toward the finish line raced the breathless runner. ("The breathless runner raced toward the finish line.")

Harcourt, Inc.

EXERCISE
5A

Circle the verb that correctly completes each sentence. Make certain that you have identified the correct subject of the sentence and that you have crossed out prepositional phrases.

1. The main crop of that region (is, are) coffee beans.

2. (Is, Are) coffee beans the region's main crop?

3. A sirloin steak with a lobster tail (costs, cost) $25.

4. One of the nation's largest booksellers (is, are) Barnes & Noble.

5. The length of women's skirts (seems, seem) to change each year.

6. In the middle of the dining room table (is, are) a large arrangement of roses and tulips.

7. Where (is, are) the claim checks for our luggage?

8. One of the dates on this contract (appears, appear) to be incorrect.

9. Where (does, do) the children's father work?

10. A popular column in the newspaper (is, are) the daily horoscopes.

11. There (is, are) a family with three small children in the hospital's waiting room.

12. The value of my stocks (varies, vary) from day to day.

13. (Has, have) the children's mother signed their report cards?

14. Here in this special diet drink (is, are) all the answers to your weight problems.

15. (Does, Do) a weight loss of five pounds per month seem reasonable for most people?

16. The results of the 2000 presidential election (was, were) not known for more than a month.

17. The main ingredient in this Lebanese recipe (tastes, taste) like chickpeas.

18. (Has, Have) the test booklets been distributed to all of the students?

19. The consumer group's main goal (is, are) lower food prices.

20. (Is, Are) the problems of the county hospital on the agenda for today's meeting?

Harcourt, Inc.

EXERCISE
5B

Some of the sentences in this exercise contain subject-verb agreement errors. Others are correct as written. If the sentence contains a subject-verb agreement error, cross out the incorrect verb and write the correct verb in its place. If the sentence is *correct*, write a *C* in the left margin.

1. Most people loves fairy tales.

2. The origin of these stories were folk tales told by special storytellers to every-one, young and old.

3. The plot of these stories have lots of action and adventures to keep the audi-ence's attention.

4. Folklorists, the people who study folktales, divides the stories into two kinds.

5. One category of folktales are cautionary tales.

6. Included in the category of cautionary tales are "Little Red Riding Hood."

7. The purpose of these tales are to warn us.

8. One of the lessons of "Little Red Riding Hood" are not to speak to strangers.

9. The pattern of magical tales differ from cautionary tales.

10. There is magical occurrences at least once in the plot.

11. The real heart of these tales are the "underdog" motif.

12. The underdog is the unsung hero, needing to find his or her proper place.

13. The underdog's role are illustrated by the story of Cinderella.

14. Sitting in the cinders are the heroine, unappreciated for all her good work.

15. In these tales, the underdog need magic to reclaim her rightful place.

16. Cinderella, along with the magic of her fairy godmother, triumph in the end.

17. Americans seem to love this underdog motif.

18. The plot of many films feature a Cinderella-like character.

19. A very commercially successful example of these kinds of films is *Pretty Woman*.

20. Fairy tales continues to be part of our life in one form or another.

CHAPTER 6

INDEFINITE PRONOUNS AS SUBJECTS

The subject pronouns we have been studying, like *she* or *it* or *they*, refer to specific, definite persons or things. This chapter is about another kind of pronoun, **indefinite pronouns,** which do not refer to a specific person or to definite things.

Rule 4. The following indefinite pronouns are **singular** and require **singular** verbs:

anybody, anyone, anything

each, each one

either, neither

everybody, everyone, everything

nobody, no one, nothing

somebody, someone, something

Everybody has his camping gear.

Anything goes.

Each of the players *knows* the ground rules.

Either of those times *is* all right with me.

Notice that in the last two sentences, the verbs agree with the singular subjects *each* and *either.* The verbs are not affected by the plural nouns in the prepositional phrases *of these players* or *of those times.*

Rule 5. Indefinite pronouns, such as the words *some, half, most,* and *all,* may take either singular or plural verbs, depending on their meaning in the context of the sentence. If these words tell **how much** of something is meant, the verb is singular; but if they tell **how many** of something is meant, the verb is plural.

Most of the milk *is* stale. (how much?)

Most of the actors *are* present. (how many?)

Some of the butter *is* missing. (how much?)

Some of the players *were* late. (how many?)

All of the fortune *goes* to the family. (how much?)

All of these items *go* to us. (how many?)

Do not confuse the words in this rule with the words *each, either,* and *neither* in Rule 4. These three words *always* require a singular verb.

Harcourt, Inc.

EXERCISE
6A

Circle the verb that correctly completes each sentence. This exercise covers only the rules from Lesson 6.

1. Each of the provinces of France (has, have) its own traditional foods and beverages.

2. Some of the provinces in northern France (has, have) been influenced by the cuisine of neighboring Germany.

3. In the province of Alsace, for example, everyone (drinks, drink) beer as well as wine.

4. Sauerkraut with sausages often (appears, appear) on Alsatian menus.

5. If someone (loves, love) good wine, the place to go is the region of Bordeaux.

6. Fine wines (is, are) the region's leading export product.

7. Some of this region's wines (is, are) used in the famous sauces that characterize Bordelaise cuisine.

8. A combination of garlic, olive oil, and tomatoes (is, are) typical of many dishes in the Mediterranean region of Provence.

9. One of the most famous Provençal dishes (is, are) a seafood stew called *bouillabaisse,* which contains all three of these ingredients.

10. (Is, Are) there anybody who hasn't heard of champagne?

11. There (is, are) other kinds of sparkling wine, but only wine from this region can be called "champagne."

12. Among the other wine-producing regions of France (is, are) Burgogne (Burgundy), which is especially famous for its fine red wines.

13. In Normandy, milk from the province's many dairy cows (produces, produce) its famous Camembert cheese.

14. There (is, are) few vineyards in this province, but the many apple orchards produce a fine cider.

15. All of the dozen or more regions of France (offers, offer) excellent food.

16. It is no wonder that many of the world's finest chefs (comes, come) from this country.

Harcourt, Inc.

EXERCISE
6B

Some of the sentences in this exercise contain subject-verb agreement errors. Others are correct as written. If the sentence contains a subject-verb agreement error, cross out the incorrect verb and write the correct verb in its place. If the sentence is correct, write a C in the margin by the sentence number. This exercise covers rules from Lesson 5 and 6.

1. Most of the students realizes the importance of study.

2. Some of their professors are providing outlines for review.

3. Any one of us are able to do well in school.

4. Each of the professors give excellent instructions.

5. Most of the food have been bought for the party.

6. All of the gifts needs to be placed on the round table.

7. At least half of the presents comes from foreign countries.

8. Most of the cake has been eaten.

9. All of the praise for the desserts go to the chef.

10. There is several members of the team here.

11. Neither of the stores have what we need.

12. Everything you desire is possible with some luck!

13. Each of the teams are arriving now.

14. All of the milk were given away to the needy children.

15. There go our new supervisor.

16. Some of the garbage are taken to the dump.

Harcourt, Inc.

17. Neither of the captains want to stop the game.

18. No one seem to understand the complexity of the situation.

19. There is far too many children in this room!

20. Most of the merchandise were delivered yesterday.

Harcourt, Inc.

CHAPTER 7

SUBJECTS UNDERSTOOD IN A SPECIAL SENSE

This chapter discusses as subjects several small groups of words that call for special attention in subject-verb agreement.

Rule 6. Some subjects, though **plural in form,** are **singular in meaning** and, therefore, require a singular verb. Such words include *news, mathematics, physics, economics, aeronautics, electronics, molasses, mumps,* and *measles.*

Economics was my least favorite class.

Mumps is a common disease among children.

Rule 7. A unit of time, weight, measurement, or **money** usually requires a singular verb because the entire amount is thought of as a single unit.

Harcourt, Inc.

Twenty *dollars is* all the money I have.

Two *pounds* of meat *feeds* four people.

Eighteen *yards* of cloth *completes* our fabric needs.

Rule 8. Collective nouns usually require singular verbs. A collective noun is a word that is singular in form but that refers to a group of people or things. Some common collective nouns are such words as *group, team, family, class, crowd,* and *committee.*

The *crowd is* very noisy.

The *committee holds* frequent meetings.

Occasionally, a collective noun may be used with a plural verb if the writer wishes to show that the members of the group are acting as separate individuals rather than as a unified body. Notice the difference in meaning between the following pair of sentences:

The *board of directors supports* the measure. (In this sentence, the *board of directors* is acting as a single, unified group.)

The *board of directors are divided* over whether to pass the measure. (In this sentence, the *board of directors* is viewed as a collection of separate individuals who, because they are not in agreement, are not acting as a unified group.)

EXERCISE
7A

Circle the verb that correctly completes each sentence. This section of the exercise covers only the rules in Lesson 7.

1. Five dollars (is, are) the price of a movie ticket for senior citizens.

2. Before inoculations were available, measles (was, were) a common childhood disease.

3. This family always (spends, spend) Thanksgiving together.

4. The County Board of Supervisors (meets, meet) every Monday morning.

5. The news from our foreign correspondents (is, are) encouraging.

6. Two cups of buttermilk (is, are) required for this recipe.

The following sentences cover rules from Lessons 5–7.

7. There (goes, go) the attorney with his famous client.

8. The attorney with his two partners (has, have) been working on this case for the last four months.

9. The fee for each attorney's services (is, are) $200 per hour.

10. Two weeks (seems, seem) like a long time to wait for the results of your test.

11. (Was, Were) most of the test items essay questions?

12. Each of the restaurants in the mall (serves, serve) a different kind of food.

13. The price of the meals at each of the restaurants (varies, vary).

14. A rice bowl with beef and vegetables (costs, cost) two dollars.

15. (Is, Are) either of the doctors working today?

16. Some of this meat (needs, need) to be cooked longer.

17. Five hundred dollars (was, were) our year-end bonus.

18. Neither of the candidates (appeals, appeal) to me very much.

19. Physics (is, are) one of the required courses for my major.

EXERCISE
7B

Some of the sentences in this exercise contain one or more subject-verb agreement errors. Others are correct as written. If the sentence contains a subject-verb agreement error, cross out the incorrect verb and write the *correct* form in its place. If the sentence is correct, write a C in the left margin. This exercise covers rules from Lessons 5–7.

1. My niece Ellen has just earned her master's degree, and there is some major career decisions facing her.

2. A degree from a well-known university, together with her extensive work experience, make her an attractive job candidate.

3. She has received job offers from companies in several different states, and each of the potential jobs appeal to her in some way.

4. Among the most important factors for Ellen are a good salary.

5. Of course, everyone want to get paid well, but financial security is especially important to Ellen.

6. Her main financial obligation are her student loans.

7. Six years are a long time to attend college, and the tuition at an Ivy League university has left her with a forty thousand dollar debt.

8. The interest rate on her loans vary from 6 to 8 percent.

9. After she leaves school, six months are all the time Ellen has before she must start to repay the loans.

10. Among Ellen's other concerns are job satisfaction.

11. Ellen knows that for beginning employees in her field, fifty hours a week constitute a normal work load.

12. Because she will have to spend long hours at the office, a combination of interesting work and a comfortable job environment are high on Ellen's list of priorities.

13. One of her potential jobs pay very well, but the location of its main and branch offices do not appeal to Ellen.

14. Ellen has always lived in large cities, and an urban location with many cultural attractions is important to her.

15. Most of her free time are spent attending concerts and plays or visiting museums and art galleries.

16. Ellen is single, and a family with a husband and several children figure prominently in her plans for the future.

17. For Ellen, another advantage of urban life are the large numbers of single professional people she can meet.

18. She faces many difficult decisions, and each of them have the potential to alter the course of her future.

19. Her whole family are watching to see what she decides to do.

Harcourt, Inc.

CHAPTER 8

SUBJECTS JOINED BY CONJUNCTIONS

Subjects joined by conjunctions require the special rules in this chapter.

Rule 9. Two subjects joined by the conjunction *and* are plural and require a plural verb.

French and *Italian are* both Romance languages.

UCLA and *USC* both *have* excellent film schools.

Rule 10. When *each, every,* or *any* is used as an adjective in front of subjects, the subjects that are modified require a singular verb. (Writers have the most trouble with this rule when the sentence has two or more subjects joined by *and,* so this rule is an exception to Rule 9, above.)

Each boy and girl under the age of five *rides* the bus free of charge.

Every Tom, Dick, and Harry *wants* to borrow money from me.

Harcourt, Inc.

Notice that the adjectives *every* and *each* make the verbs in the sentences singular even though each sentence has more than one subject.

Rule 11. Two singular subjects joined by the conjunctions *or* or *nor* are singular and require a singular verb.

> Neither *John* nor *Harold knows* the telephone number.
>
> *Monday* or *Tuesday is* my parents' anniversary.

Rule 12. If both a singular and a plural subject are joined by *or* or *nor,* the subject that is closer to the verb determines whether the verb is singular or plural.

> Either two *onions* or a *clove* of garlic *is* necessary for this recipe.
>
> Either a *clove* of garlic or two *onions are* necessary for this recipe.
>
> *Is* a *clove* of garlic or two *onions* necessary for this recipe?
>
> *Are* two *onions* or a *clove* of garlic necessary for this recipe?

> (Note: In the final two sentences, it is the *helping* verb that agrees with the subject.)

EXERCISE
8A

Circle the verb that correctly completes each sentence. This section of the exercise covers only the rules in Lesson 8.

1. An exciting story line and excellent acting (has, have) made the new television series a success.

2. Every student and faculty member (participates, participate) in the school's homecoming activities.

3. Either you or your attorney (has, have) the papers I need.

4. (Do, Does) your attorney or you have the papers I need?

5. Either the doctor or a physician's assistant (takes, take) your medical history.

6. The style of a dress and its fabric (determines, determine) its price.

7. Neither her husband nor her children (knows, know) her real age.

8. A soup or a salad (is, are) included with your meal.

Sentences 9–20 cover the rules in Lessons 5–8.

9. There (is, are) a choice of salads on this menu.

10. Each of the subjects in a sentence (has, have) to agree with its verb.

11. Two weeks of vacation never (seems, seem) long enough.

12. A bouquet of flowers or a box of candy (makes, make) a nice Valentine's Day gift.

13. Some of his money (has, have) been invested in technology stocks.

14. Either a money market account or a bond fund (is, are) a safer investment.

15. (Does, Do) either of the libraries stay open in the evening?

16. Some of the store's furniture (is, are) on sale this week.

17. Cornish hens or a turkey (is, are) our usual Thanksgiving dinner.

18. (Does, Do) a turkey or Cornish hens need to be stuffed before being roasted?

19. (Is, Are) economics a prerequisite for business administration courses?

20. Among the favorite attractions in Southern California (is, are) the Universal Studios tour.

Harcourt, Inc.

EXERCISE
8B

Some of the sentences in this exercise contain subject-verb agreement errors. Others are correct as written. If the sentence contains a subject-verb agreement error, cross out the incorrect verb and write the *correct* form in its place. If the sentence is correct, write C in the left margin. This exercise covers rules from Lessons 5–8.

1. The aging of the American population and our longer lifespans has made retirement an important social issue.

2. In the past, sixty-five years were considered old, and a person that age could expect to live fewer than ten additional years.

3. Today, a longer lifespan, together with advances in health care, give retirees new choices on how to spend their later years.

4. Relaxing at home or visiting senior citizens' centers are no longer enough for many seniors.

5. Instead, opportunities for volunteer work attract many retirees.

6. Tutoring children in school or volunteering in hospitals offer seniors a chance to remain involved in society.

7. In the words of one senior, "Staying active and helping others gives me a reason to wake up in the morning."

8. Among other ways to remain active is continuing education classes for seniors.

9. In the Elder Hostel program, for example, a group of seniors live on a college campus and attend special seminars.

10. Sharing a small dormitory room and eating in a college cafeteria is a new experience for some seniors.

11. A wider choice of living arrangements are also available to today's senior citizens.

12. The growth of "retirement villages" give seniors a chance to live among people their own age.

13. A variety of recreational activities and the availability of on-site medical care attracts many retirees to these communities.

14. For other seniors, staying in their own homes and in their own communities are important.

15. A variation on dating services for the young match seniors with compatible housemates.

16. Sharing a house and dividing living expenses enables seniors to afford to remain in their own homes.

17. In addition, no longer do a long illness or a serious injury mean that they must leave their own homes and enter nursing facilities.

18. The availability of visiting nurses and home health aides enable many seniors to receive medical care at home.

19. Seeing a seventy-year-old couple traveling across the country in a recreational vehicle or having a ninety-year-old living independently no longer surprise us.

20. Perhaps an even wider range of opportunities for life after retirement await those of us who are still young.

UNIT REVIEW

SUBJECT-VERB AGREEMENT

Correct any subject-verb agreement errors that you find in the following essay by crossing out the incorrect verb and writing in the correct form. It may help you to underline all the subjects in the essay *once* and all the verbs *twice* before you try to identify errors in agreement.

Among the most valuable of all gems are the diamond. The word *diamond* comes from the Greek *adamas,* meaning "indestructible," for diamonds are the hardest of all gems. The hardness of diamonds enable them to be polished to a brilliance unequaled by other gems. The scarcity of diamonds, together with their hardness and brilliance, account for their great value.

One of the major factors affecting the value of diamonds are their weight. The weight of diamonds is measured in carats. Each of a diamond's carats weigh 200 milligrams (1/142nd of an ounce). The weight of the largest diamond ever found were 3,106 carats.

The clarity of diamonds also influence their worth. Hardly anyone owns a "perfect" diamond, for most diamonds contain some flaws. A small spot of carbon or a bubble in the stone reduce a diamond's quality. Similarly, a crack or small chips lowers its value.

The appearance of diamonds are directly affected by the way in which they are cut. In their natural state, rough diamonds seldom seem beautiful. Some diamond crystals have a dull coating; others resembles pieces of broken glass. Each of these stones have to be cut and polished. A maximum of brilliance and a minimum of flaws is the goal of the diamond cutter.

The color of diamonds vary widely. "Colorless" diamonds brings the highest price. Actually, few diamonds are colorless; some amount of yellow or brown color occur in most stones.

Thus, the value of diamonds depend on the "four C's": carat, clarity, cut, and color.

UNIT 3

IDENTIFYING AND PUNCTUATING THE MAIN TYPES OF SENTENCES

C H A P T E R 9

COMPOUND SENTENCES

compound sentence, a very common sentence pattern, contains *at least two subjects and two verbs,* usually arranged in an S-V/S-V pattern. For example,

```
 S    V                    S    V
Bob wrecked his car last week, and now he rides the bus to work.
```

```
 S    V                    S    V
Nina lived in Italy for two years, so she speaks Italian fluently.
```

In grammar, the term **compound** means "having two or more parts." Thus, a sentence may have a **compound subject;** for example, "The *husband* and his *wife* were at the opera." Or, a sentence may have a **compound verb;** for example, "The man *rode* his bike and *sped* down the street." Do not confuse a sentence with a **compound subject** or a **compound verb** with a **compound sentence.**

Harcourt, Inc.

77

A compound sentence can be divided into two parts, each of which can be a separate sentence by itself.

Bob wrecked his car last week.   +   Now he rides the bus to work

Nina lived in Italy for two years.   +   She speaks Italian very fluently.

Because a compound sentence can be divided into *two* separate sentences, each half of a compound sentence must contain at least one subject and one verb. Therefore, each half of a compound sentence is a **clause.** A clause is a group of words that contains both a subject and a verb. (In contrast, a group of words that does not contain both a subject and a verb is called a **phrase,** as in a prepositional phrase.) A clause that can stand alone as a complete sentence is called an **independent clause.** Because each clause in a compound sentence can stand alone as a complete sentence, each clause must be independent. In other words,

A compound sentence consists of at least two independent clauses joined together to form a single sentence.

There are two ways to join independent clauses to form a compound sentence. The most frequently used method is to put a conjunction between the clauses. A **conjunction** is a word that joins words or groups of words. In grammar, the word *coordinate* means "of equal importance." Therefore, the conjunctions that are used in compound sentences are called **coordinating conjunctions** because they join two groups of words that are of equal grammatical importance. (They are both independent clauses.) The following coordinating conjunctions are used to join the clauses of compound sentences:

and

but

for (when it means *because*)

nor

or

so

yet

You should *memorize* these coordinating conjunctions because later you will have to be able to distinguish between them and the connecting words that are used to form other kinds of sentences.

Harcourt, Inc.

In the following sentences, underline the subjects of the compound sentences *once* and the verbs *twice,* and circle the coordinating conjunction that joins the clauses. Notice that a comma *precedes* the coordinating conjunction.

The president entered the room, and the band began to play "Hail to the Chief."

She diets constantly, but her weight remains the same.

I rarely prepare casseroles, for my family refuses to eat them.

We must hurry, or we will miss the first part of the movie.

He can't help you, nor can I.

(Notice that when the conjunction *nor* is used to join two independent clauses, the pattern becomes S-V/V-S: My coat isn't here, nor is my hat.)

The defendant was ill, so the trial was postponed.

He earns only $800 a month, yet he lives quite comfortably.

Construct compound sentences of your own, using the coordinating conjunctions listed below to join your clauses. Underline the subject of each clause *once* and the verb *twice.* (You may construct a clause that has more than one subject and/or more than one verb, but each clause must have *at least* one subject and one verb.)

_____, and _____

_____, but _____

_____, for _____

_____, or _____

The second way to join the clauses in a compound sentence is to use a semicolon (;) *in place of both the comma and the coordinating conjunction.* For example,

She could not find her keys; they must have fallen somewhere.

Mark is always late for work; he oversleeps every morning.

Compound sentences constructed with semicolons occur less frequently than compound sentences constructed with coordinating conjunctions because some type of connecting word is usually needed to show the relationship between the clauses. For example, without a coordinating conjunction the logical relationship between the two clauses in the following sentence might be confusing.

My grandfather has lived in the United States for fifty years; he has never learned to speak English.

If, however, you replace the semicolon with a coordinating conjunction, the relationship between the clauses becomes clear.

> My grandfather has lived in the United States for fifty years, but he has never learned to speak English.

It is all right to use the semicolon by itself between the clauses of a compound sentence, but do so only when the relationship between the clauses is clear without a connecting word.

Construct two compound sentences of your own, using semicolons to join the clauses. Underline the subjects *once* and the verbs *twice*. Make certain that each clause has at least one subject and one verb.

_____; _____

_____; _____

Another common way to show the relationship between the clauses of a compound sentence is to use a **conjunctive adverb**, like *however*, in the second clause. Notice that a *semicolon* is required between the clauses. A comma follows the conjunctive adverb.

> We all studied quite hard; however, the test was more difficult than we had expected.

Conjunctive adverbs are especially frequent in formal language, where expressing the precise relationship between ideas is the goal. Here are the most frequently used conjunctive adverbs:

also	incidentally	nonetheless
anyway	indeed	otherwise
besides	instead	still
consequently	likewise	then
finally	meanwhile	therefore
furthermore	moreover	thus
hence	nevertheless	
however	next	

A conjunctive adverb gets its double name from the fact that it does two things at once: It connects, like other **conjunctions,** and it modifies, like other **adverbs.** Because it is adverbial, it can be located in many places in its own clause. Because it can move around in the second clause and does not always come *exactly between* the two clauses (like coordinating conjunctions), it does not necessarily act as a

Harcourt, Inc.

signal to readers that they are coming to the second half of a compound sentence. For these reasons, the strong signal of a semicolon marks the end of the first clause.

Bob loved to surf; therefore, he lived near the beach.

Bob loved to surf; he, therefore, lived near the beach.

Bob loved to surf; he lived near the beach, therefore.

Roberto drives carefully; his brother, however, does not.

(Notice that the conjunctive adverb is always "set off" with a comma, or two commas, in its own clause.) Construct three compound sentences of your own that use conjunctive adverbs. Try putting the conjunctive adverb in several different places in the second clause.

1._____

2._____

3._____

(Did you remember to "set off" the conjunctive adverb with one or two commas?)

As you can see from the sentences that you have constructed in this lesson, the following punctuation rules apply to compound sentences:

1. If the clauses in a compound sentence are joined by a coordinating conjunction, place a comma *before* (to the left of) the conjunction.

This sentence is compound, and it contains a comma.

You may have learned that it is not necessary to use commas in short compound sentences (for example, "He's a Scorpio and I'm a Libra."). Although this is true, not everyone agrees on how short a "short" compound sentence is, so if you are in doubt, it is safer to use a comma. All the sentences in the exercises for this unit will be "long" compound sentences and should have a comma before the conjunction.

2. Although a compound sentence may contain more than one coordinating conjunction, the comma is placed before the conjunction that joins the clauses.

Jan and I attended the same college, and now we work for the same company.

3. If the clauses in a compound sentence are *not* joined by a coordinating conjunction, place a semicolon between the clauses. If the clauses are joined by a conjunctive adverb, the adverb must also be *followed* by a comma.

I don't have my book with me; I must have left it at home.

We hurried to the theater; however, the film was over.

This sentence has two independent clauses; it is, therefore, a compound sentence.

The following sentence patterns do *not* require commas because they are simple (meaning that they contain only one clause) rather than compound.

S-V-V	He ordered a baked potato but was served French fries instead. (no comma)
S-S-V	My uncle and aunt live in Boston. (no comma)
S-S-V-V	My cousin and I went to England and stayed there for two months. (no comma)

To review, the two patterns for punctuating a compound sentence are:

clause + comma + coordinating conjunction + clause

We went to a play, and next we had some dinner.

clause + semicolon + clause

We didn't enjoy the movie; it was boring.

I love to draw; however, I have little artistic talent.

Harcourt, Inc.

EXERCISE
9A

Add commas and semicolons to the following sentences wherever they are needed. If a sentence needs no additional punctuation (in other words, if the sentence is simple rather than compound), label it C for correct in the left margin.

1. Pumpkins are vegetables native to the New World therefore they were unknown in Europe before the Age of Exploration.

2. The Indians of New England raised pumpkins in their cornfields and the early English settlers learned how to eat pumpkins from then.

3. The early settlers did not have ovens so they baked whole pumpkins in the ashes of their fireplaces.

4. The cooked pumpkins were cut open and served with maple syrup or honey.

5. Later, the pumpkins were stuffed with milk and spices before baking this dish was the ancestor of the pumpkin pie.

6. It is difficult to believe but the settlers even brewed a beer from pumpkins.

7. Slices of pumpkin were strung on thread and dried they were then eaten like potato chips.

8. The settlers often relied on homemade medicines to treat their ailments and crushed pumpkin seeds were used as a remedy for stomachaches.

9. Pumpkins were sent back to Europe but they were not popular there for a long time except as food for animals.

10. Today, pumpkins are not just a food item for they are also used as holiday decorations.

Harcourt, Inc.

11. The Irish brought the custom of making jack-o'-lanterns to the United States however in Ireland turnips were used to make lanterns.

12. Pumpkins make larger and more impressive lanterns so they gradually replaced turnips at Halloween.

13. The pumpkin is a humble vegetable yet it plays an important role in two of our holidays.

14. Do you carve a Halloween jack-o'-lantern and does your family eat pumpkin pie at Thanksgiving?

Harcourt, Inc.

Exercise
9B

Add commas and semicolons to the following sentences wherever they are needed. If a sentence needs no additional punctuation (in other words, if the sentence is simple rather than compound), label it C for correct in the left margin.

1. In most countries, few high school students have part-time jobs instead they devote their time and energy to studying.

2. Of course, students in other parts of the world spend more hours in school than American students so they have less free time for jobs.

3. Part-time jobs are important to many American teenagers for they use their salaries to support their lifestyle.

4. Older teenagers often have cars therefore they need to pay for expenses like gasoline and insurance.

5. Most American teenagers date and going out on a date can be very expensive.

6. The price of a movie ticket, for example, seems to increase each year in addition it is necessary to pay for parking and snacks.

7. Clothing is another expense many teenagers pay for some or all of their wardrobe.

8. In some cases, a teenager's salary is necessary to supplement the family's income and the student may have no alternative but to work.

9. The responsibilities of working and managing their own money can be a valuable experience for teenagers however part-time jobs may have a negative effect on the students' performance in school.

10. Working after school leaves too few hours for rest and study and students may come to school too tired to learn well.

11. Tired students often seem unresponsive in fact they sometimes fall asleep during the class.

12. Working students may neglect to do their homework assignments or they may do them carelessly.

13. It is often easier to neglect school than to neglect a job for schools don't usually "fire" students.

14. Americans place a high value on both earning money and education thus it may be difficult to find an easy solution to this problem.

15. Currently, some students work twenty hours a week or more and still carry a full load of classes.

16. A partial solution might be to allow high school students to work but to limit their jobs to work on weekends.

17. Working on weekends seems like an ideal solution however few jobs offer this option.

18. Are part-time jobs a problem only for high school students or do they cause difficulties for college students too?

Harcourt, Inc.

CHAPTER 10

COMPLEX SENTENCES

There are two kinds of clauses, independent and dependent. As you have seen in Lesson 9, **independent clauses** can stand alone as complete sentences. For example,

I was ill.

We loved the play.

A **dependent clause,** however, *cannot* stand alone as a complete sentence. Instead, it must be attached to, or *depend* on, an *independent* clause to form a grammatically complete sentence and to express a complete idea. Notice that the following dependent clauses are not complete sentences.

When he comes over . . .

If we come to the play . . .

Before we saw the movie . . .

These clauses seem incomplete because they are actually only part of a sentence. Using the first of the following sentences as a model, change each dependent clause into a complete sentence by adding an appropriate *independent* clause.

Harcourt, Inc.

87

When he comes over, *we watch television.*

If we come to the play, _____

_____

Before we saw the movie, _____

_____

You have now constructed two complex sentences. A **complex sentence** contains both independent and dependent clauses. (In contrast, a **compound sentence** contains only *independent* clauses.)

Every dependent clause begins with a subordinating conjunction. A **conjunction** joins words or groups of words. The conjunctions that begin dependent clauses are called **subordinating conjunctions** because the word *subordinate* means "of lesser importance." Grammatically speaking, a dependent clause is "less important" than an independent clause because it cannot stand alone as a complete sentence. In contrast, the conjunctions that you used in the previous lesson to form compound sentences are called **coordinating conjunctions** because *coordinate* means "of equal importance." Because both of the clauses in a compound sentence are independent, both clauses are "of equal importance."

The type of dependent clause that you will be studying in this lesson is called an **adverb clause** because, like other adverbs, an adverb clause describes a verb (or sometimes an adjective or an adverb). It is the same kind of clause that you worked with in Lesson 2. The subordinating conjunctions used to begin adverb clauses describe verbs by telling *how, when, where, why,* or *under what conditions* the action occurs.

how: as if, as though

when: after, as, as soon as, before, until, when, whenever, while

where: where, wherever

why: because, in order that, since, so that

under what conditions: although, as long as, even though, if, though, unless

Read the following sentences. A slanted line indicates the point at which each sentence divides into two separate clauses. Underline the subject of each clause *once* and the verb *twice.* Circle the subordinating conjunction.

While we studied, / he watched TV.

I babysat / so that they could go to a movie.

As long as we communicate, / we will remain friends.

Now examine the clause in each sentence that contains the circled subordinating conjunction.

Harcourt, Inc.

The clause that contains the subordinating conjunction is the dependent clause.

Notice that in a complex sentence, the dependent clause may be either the first or the second clause in the sentence.

When *Julia sings,* she is very happy.

Rick finds time to exercise *after he finishes work.*

In most cases, the adverb clauses in a complex sentence are *reversible.* That is, the sentence has the same basic meaning no matter which clause comes first. For example,

When he takes the train, he usually reads his books.

He usually reads his books *when he takes the train.*

or

If we go on vacation, we will have lots of fun.

We will have lots of fun *if we go on vacation.*

However, the order of the clauses in a complex sentence does affect the punctuation of the sentence.

1. If the **dependent** clause is the first clause in the sentence, it is followed by a comma.

   Before she performed at the club, Stephanie welcomed her guests.

2. If the **independent** clause is the first clause in the sentence, no comma is needed.
   Stephanie welcomed her guests *before she performed at the club.*

Punctuate the following complex sentences. First circle the subordinating conjunction in each sentence, and draw a slanted line between the clauses.

After we eat dinner we're going to see a movie.

The child carries her teddy bear with her wherever she goes.

If it doesn't rain the crops will be ruined.

As soon as I finish painting my apartment I'll help you paint yours.

EXERCISE
10A

The following sentences are **complex.** First, underline the dependent clause in each sentence. Then add a comma to the sentence if it is necessary. If a sentence needs no additional punctuation, label it C for *correct.*

1. As soon as humans learned to write they needed to find ways to record their writing.

2. Before paper was invented people wrote on clay tablets.

3. Marks were cut into the surface of the tablet while the clay was still wet.

4. After the tablet dried the marks were preserved in the clay.

5. Although clay was cheap and easily available clay tablets were bulky and difficult to store.

6. The ancient Egyptians found a better way to record their writing because they made a kind of paper from the papyrus plant.

7. The stalks of the papyrus were cut into slices, soaked, and pressed until they became flat sheets.

8. Papyrus sheets could be stored easily because they could be rolled into scrolls.

Sentences 9–19 are a mixture of **compound** and **complex** sentences. Add commas and semicolons to the sentences wherever they are needed. If a sentence needs no additional punctuation, label it C for *Correct.*

9. The Greeks and the Romans used papyrus too but they also wrote on wooden tablets.

10. The tablets were covered with wax and words were cut into the wax with a sharp stylus.

11. If a writer wanted to reuse a tablet he simply scraped off the top layer of wax.

12. The first real paper was invented in China around A.D. 100 it was made from the inner bark of mulberry trees.

13. Later on, rags were also used in making paper because they were more easily available than mulberry bark.

14. From China, paper-making techniques spread to the Middle East because Arab traders traveled between the two regions.

15. When Arabs invaded Spain in the seventh century they brought paper-making techniques to Europe for the first time.

16. For many centuries, paper was made by hand and this made it very expensive.

17. Now, modern mills manufacture tons of paper each day so paper has become an inexpensive, disposable item.

18. The popularity of personal computers and the use of e-mail were supposed to reduce our need for paper however this doesn't seem to have happened yet.

19. Therefore, people are being encouraged to recycle paper whenever they can to save trees and to reduce the amount of trash in landfills.

Harcourt, Inc.

EXERCISE
10B

The essay below includes simple, compound, and complex sentences, but they are not always punctuated correctly. Correct all punctuation errors.

Most of us have grown up around some form of pet. Whether it was puppies or kittens or frogs or tropical fish animals have played an important role in our childhoods. At times, we may have taken these pets for granted and assumed that animals exist primarily for the convenience of humans. However, things seem to be changing because some people have begun to talk about animal rights.

One big change has been protests against the wearing of fur coats. Because animal rights activists have made the wearing and selling of these coats so controversial they have almost run furriers out of business. Other people object to such tactics because they restrict the rights of businesses to sell their products and of people to choose their apparel. Fake furs may provide a partial solution if customers are willing to substitute imitations for the real things.

Another effect of the animal rights movement has been a growing awareness of the need to protect endangered species. These species may be threatened with extinction unless we intervene. In America, the native wolf, California condor, and Southern red fox have all been helped by being protected and their numbers are steadily increasing. However, endangered species of animals in our country and in other countries are still threatened because they are being killed by poachers for their skins, horns, and tusks. Because animal parts are often exported to other countries worldwide cooperation will be necessary to save endangered species.

The new emphasis on animal rights may also have made people more aware of how they treat their pets. People are more willing to give their pets better medical care and pet owners often spend a great deal of money to keep their animals healthy. There are laws that protect pets from physical abuse and shelters have been established to rescue and treat abused or unwanted pets. An attempt is often made to adopt these animals they are no longer just routinely destroyed.

The only adverse effect of the animal rights movement has been its effect on medical research. Because medical experiments often use animals as research subjects limiting the use of animals may delay the development of new drugs and surgical procedures. However, to animal rights activists, such worries are a form of "speciesism." This belief makes human rights more important than those of any other species. These activists also oppose experiments on animals because research animals are sometimes subjected to very painful procedures. The animals may also be kept in small cages, with no access to exercise or the company of other animals. The goal of animal rights advocates is for experiments to be done on computer models or on human volunteers. This issue is still controversial so we cannot say how it will finally be decided.

CHAPTER 11

AVOIDING RUN-ON SENTENCES AND COMMA SPLICES

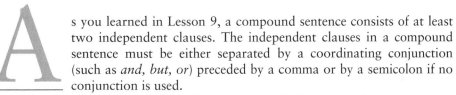

s you learned in Lesson 9, a compound sentence consists of at least two independent clauses. The independent clauses in a compound sentence must be either separated by a coordinating conjunction (such as *and, but, or*) preceded by a comma or by a semicolon if no conjunction is used.

Failure to separate two independent clauses results in an error known as a **run-on sentence.** The following are examples of run-on sentences.

I don't play tennis well I have a poor backhand.

The next game is at our school we want to go to it.

Run-on sentences are very serious errors. They are not only confusing to the reader but also indicate that the writer cannot tell where one sentence ends and another begins.

There are three ways to correct a run-on sentence.

Harcourt, Inc.

1. Divide the run-on into two separate sentences, ending each with a period. (If the sentences are questions, end them with question marks.)

I don't play tennis well. I have a poor backhand.

The next game is at our school. We want to go to it.

Although this method produces grammatically correct sentences, an essay written completely in such short, simple sentences creates the choppy effect of an elementary school reading text. Therefore, you should also consider using the two other methods of correcting run-ons.

2. Change the run-on to a **compound sentence** by separating the clauses with a semicolon or with a coordinating conjunction preceded by a comma.

I don't play tennis well; I have a poor backhand.

or

I don't play tennis well, *for* I have a poor backhand.

The next game is at our school; therefore, we want to go to it.

or

The next game is at our school, *so* we want to go to it.

As you learned previously, the relationship between the two clauses in a compound sentence is often clearer if a conjunction is used rather than a semicolon.

3. Change the run-on to a complex sentence by placing a subordinating conjunction before one of the clauses.

Because I have a poor backhand, I don't play tennis well.

Because the next game is at our school, we want to go to it.

Another very common error is the comma splice. Unlike a run-on, in which two independent clauses are run together with no punctuation, a **comma splice** consists of two independent clauses joined with *not enough* punctuation—that is, with only a comma (and *no* coordinating conjunction). The following are examples of comma splices.

I didn't finish the novel, it was boring.

Bob needs a new car, he can't afford to buy one now.

Harcourt, Inc.

A comma by itself is *not* a strong enough punctuation mark to separate two independent clauses. Only periods and semicolons can be used without conjunctions to separate independent clauses. Comma splices can be corrected by the same three methods used for correcting run-on sentences.

1. Divide the comma splice into two separate sentences.

   I didn't finish the novel. It was boring.

   Bob needs a new car. He can't afford to buy one now.

2. Change the comma splice into a **compound sentence** by separating the clauses with either a coordinating conjunction *and* a comma or with a semicolon.

   I didn't finish the novel, *for* it was boring.

or

   I didn't finish the novel; it was boring.

   Bob needs a new car, *but* he can't afford to buy one now.

or

   Bob needs a new car; however, he can't afford to buy one now.

3. Change the comma splice into a **complex sentence** by placing a subordinating conjunction before one of the clauses.

   I didn't finish the novel *because* it was boring.

   Although Bob needs a new car, he can't afford to buy one now.

Remember that if the dependent clause (the clause continuing the subordinating conjunction) is the first clause in the sentence, it should be followed by a comma.

Correct the following run-on sentences and comma splices:

I would like to visit Hawaii I have many relatives there.

All my sisters have blue eyes I do not.

Gary is used to cold weather, he grew up in Minnesota.

They are always in debt they have too many credit cards.

Sue has many problems, she always manages to look cheerful.

EXERCISE
11A

Correct all the run-on sentences and comma splices. If a sentence is neither a run-on nor a comma splice, label it *C* for *correct* in the left margin.

1. The United States has a large immigrant population, schools need to find effective ways to teach children English.

2. Bilingual education is a popular method of teaching children English it has both advantages and disadvantages.

3. In a bilingual classroom, instruction is in both English and the students' native language the teacher speaks both languages fluently.

4. The students and the teacher can easily communicate with each other, they have a common language.

5. Students can study academic subjects, such as science, in their own language they do not fall behind in other subjects while learning English.

6. Ideally, students will maintain proficiency in their native language as well as learning English, they will end up being truly bilingual.

7. However, students in a bilingual classroom must divide their time between two languages it may take them longer to master English.

8. In addition, school districts often have a shortage of bilingual teachers not many teachers are fluent in two languages.

9. Most bilingual classes serve Spanish-speaking students, students who speak less common languages often have trouble finding a bilingual instructor.

Harcourt, Inc.

10. For example, a first-grade class in Hollywood, California, may have ten Spanish-speaking students, five students from Korea, six from Armenia, five from Russia, and several from Ethiopia and Bangladesh in a case like this, it is impossible to put each student into a bilingual classroom.

11. Another approach to teaching English is English as a Second Language or ESL, in this method all the classroom instruction is in English.

12. Sometimes a bilingual teacher's aide may help beginning students the emphasis is on teaching English, not on maintaining the students' native languages.

13. Students in an ESL class hear English all day long, young students, in particular, often make rapid progress in learning English.

14. Older students, however, may take several years to learn English meanwhile, they may fall behind in their other subjects.

15. Students in an ESL class do not read and write in their native languages, they may end up being literate only in English.

16. Graduates of ESL classes sometimes have trouble communicating with their parents and other adults their native language remains at a child's level.

17. On the other hand, many immigrant parents want their children to learn English as fast as possible these parents favor ESL classes.

18. There is a lot of controversy about the best way to teach children English experts on the subject often disagree in their opinions.

EXERCISE
11B

Each of the paragraphs in the essay below contains comma splices and run-on sentences. Correct these errors using the methods you have learned from this and previous lessons.

The presidential election of 2000 will be remembered as the closest election in the nation's history up to this point, it took more than a month after election day to choose a winner even then the results were contested by some.

Because the election was so close, it was impossible to pick a winner until the results in Florida, Oregon, Iowa, and Wisconsin were complete, even these results were not complete by the end of election day because absentee ballots had to be counted. As it finally turned out, Al Gore, the Democratic presidential candidate, won the overall popular vote by about 300,000 votes, however, his opponent, George W. Bush, the Republican candidate, won the electoral college vote and was inaugurated as president on January 21, 2001.

This election made Americans very aware of the institution of the electoral college. The electoral college is made up of representatives from each state, these representatives are selected by their political parties at state conventions they are often asked to sign a pledge binding them to vote for their party's candidate. On election day the voters elect one party's slate of electors by voting for that party's candidate, the winning slate of electors is then officially designated as the electors for that state.

Harcourt, Inc.

In forty-eight of the fifty-one "states" (the District of Columbia serving as the fifty-first "state" and also possessing electors), the slate of electors is chosen entirely from the party that wins the largest number of votes in that state's presidential election. If, for example, the Republican candidate in Iowa wins 50.1 percent of that state's popular vote, Iowa chooses a Republican slate of electors, all of the state's votes go to the Republican candidate. In Maine and Nebraska, this vote can be split and some of the votes can go to candidates from each party.

The electors from each state then meet and cast their vote, those votes are sealed and sent by December 27 in the year of the election to the president of the Senate and the archivist of the United States and other state and federal officials on January 6 these votes are counted by a joint session of Congress.

The electoral college was originally created so that the states would have more independence in electing the president, the electoral college is an affirmation of state's rights it also honors the idea that the United States is not a pure democracy but a republic. A republic operates by electing representatives to carry out the people's wishes rather than by referring in all cases directly back to the people.

Though the electoral college has been criticized throughout its history, it will be difficult to change it eliminating the electoral college would require an amendment to the United States Constitution.

Harcourt, Inc.

12

CORRECTING FRAGMENTS

The basic unit of expression in written English is the sentence. As you already know, *a sentence must contain at least one independent clause.*

If you take a group of words that is *not* a complete sentence and punctuate it as though it were a complete sentence, you have created a **sentence fragment.** In other words, you have written only a piece—a fragment—of a sentence rather than a complete sentence.

As you can see. These groups of words. Are fragments.

Because semicolons and periods are usually interchangeable, fragments may also be created by misusing semicolons. If you look carefully at the following two groups of words, you will see that they should form a single complex sentence that needs only a comma, and not a semicolon.

As you can see; wrong punctuation may be confusing.

As you can see, wrong punctuation may be confusing.

Harcourt, Inc.

Although fragments occur frequently in speech and occasionally in informal writing, they are generally not acceptable in classroom writing and should be avoided in formal writing situations.

There are two types of fragments: **dependent clauses** and **phrases.**

As you have already learned (Lesson 10), a dependent clause cannot stand alone as a complete sentence. It must be attached to an independent clause to form a complex sentence.

Therefore, any dependent clause that is separated from its main clause by a period or semicolon is a fragment.

Below are several examples of this type of fragment.

When we arrived at the theater. The movie had already begun.

When we arrived at the theater; the movie had already begun.

We'll miss our plane. If we don't hurry.

We'll miss our plane; if we don't hurry.

Eliminate the dependent clause fragments in the following paragraph by punctuating them correctly.

Because we are trying to eat more healthful food. We are buying more fruits and vegetables. The problem occurs. Whenever we go to a restaurant. At the restaurant, desserts tempt us; although we have the best of intentions to eat only healthful foods. If we were at home; we would never think of eating pies and ice cream. Because the menu is so intriguing. We wind up ordering things no one would consider to be healthy. When we order banana splits and ice cream; it isn't healthy, but we sure are happy.

Are you remembering to punctuate each dependent clause according to its location? As you learned in Lesson 10, if the *dependent* clause is the first clause in a sentence, it should be followed by a comma. If the *independent* clause is the first clause in a sentence, no comma is needed.

The second type of fragment is the **phrase.** Because a phrase is defined as a group of words that does not contain both a subject and a verb, a phrase obviously cannot be a complete sentence. *All phrases are fragments.* Study the following types of fragments, and notice the way each phrase has been changed from a fragment into a complete sentence.

Harcourt, Inc.

FRAGMENT—NO SUBJECT	Had seen that film.
SENTENCE	*We* had seen that film.
FRAGMENT—NO VERB	The children on the bus.
SENTENCE	The children *rode* on the bus.
FRAGMENT—INCOMPLETE VERB (-ING FORM)	Kevin attending a conference.
SENTENCE	Kevin *was attending* a conference.

(An -ing main verb must be preceded by a helping verb.)

or

Kevin *attended* a conference.

(Change the -ing verb to a main verb.)

FRAGMENT—INCOMPLETE VERB (PAST PARTICIPLE)	The garden filled with flowers.
SENTENCE	The garden *is filled* with flowers.

(To be a main verb, a past participle must be preceded by a helping verb. See Lesson 25 for an explanation and a list of past participles.)

FRAGMENT—INFINITIVE	To do well in school.
SENTENCE	*Students must study* hard to do well in school.
FRAGMENT—PARTICIPIAL PHRASE	Being a good friend.
SENTENCE	Being a good friend *takes* a lot of hard work.

The following groups of words are fragments because they lack either a subject or a verb or because they have an incomplete verb. Rewrite each fragment so that it becomes a complete sentence.

The weather being much too cold for swimming.

Ate a pizza for lunch yesterday.

Praying for a good turnout.

The candidate knowing that his lead would not hold.

A present sent by air mail.

The house damaged by the tornado.

The city's new subway system.

When you are writing a composition, be careful not to separate a phrase from the rest of the sentence to which it belongs.

INCORRECT	I'm looking for a small puppy. With floppy white ears.
CORRECT	I'm looking for a small puppy with floppy white ears.
INCORRECT	Wanting to do well; he studied all night.
CORRECT	Wanting to do well, he studied all night.

Rewrite the following items so that any fragments are correctly joined with the sentences to which they belong.

I burned my hand. While frying chicken for dinner.

Pleased with the pianist's performance. The audience demanded an encore.

Susan lay sleeping on the beach. From noon until three o'clock.

To summarize: **Phrases** are sentence fragments because they do not contain both a subject and a complete verb. (In other words, they are not **clauses.**) **Dependent clauses** are fragments because they are not *independent* clauses. This is simply another way of stating the most basic rule of sentence construction:

Every sentence must contain at least one independent clause.

EXERCISE
12A

Correct any fragments you find in the following exercise. If an item contains no fragments, label it C for *correct*.

1. When most Americans think of Native Americans. They picture the Indians of the Great Plains.

2. Countless painters having portrayed these tribes. As fearless warriors and great hunters.

3. Actually, the great age of the Plains Indians lasted for only two centuries.

4. Starting with the introduction of the horse at the beginning of the eighteenth century and ending with the defeat of the Native Americans by the United States Army at the end of the nineteenth century.

5. Before the Spanish brought horses to North America. Some Plains Indians tribes were already nomadic buffalo hunters.

6. However, their mobility was limited. Because they traveled on foot and had only dogs as pack animals.

7. Dogs hauling burdens and people on foot carrying their belongings could travel only five or six miles a day.

8. Moving camp was a difficult task. Especially for the aged, the women, and the children.

9. Horses gradually spread from Mexico and the Southwest to the Great Plains. Through intertribal trading.

10. After a tribe acquired horses. Its way of life changed.

Harcourt, Inc.

11. The most important changes being increased mobility, easier methods for hunting buffalo, and more opportunities for waging war against other tribes.

12. The Plains Indians perfected a lifestyle based on the horse. But were eventually forced off their lands by the westward expansion of the United States.

EXERCISE
12B

The paragraphs in the essay below contain *comma splices*, *run-ons*, and *fragments*. Correct these errors using the methods you have learned from this and previous lessons.

Although many adult Americans are trying to control their weight. Obesity is increasing among American children. Experts referring to this trend as the "supersizing" of the nation's children.

There are several causes for this problem. One being that children now consume about 200 calories more each day than they did a decade ago. Unfortunately, a lot of these extra calories come from unhealthy snacks. Like soft drinks, candy, and other "junk food." Besides being fattening. These foods are lacking in nutritional value.

In addition to consuming more calories, children get less exercise. Because they spend much of their free time on sedentary activities. Grade-school children spending an average of twenty hours a week watching television. Although the time children spend on television is actually decreasing. It is being replaced by hours devoted to computers and video games. Children used to exercise at school now many schools have reduced or eliminated their physical education programs. To spend more time on preparing for standardized tests.

Obesity in children is more than a cosmetic problem it can also cause medical problems. Pediatricians finding an alarming increase in diabetes and high blood pressure among children. These diseases formerly common mainly among adults. Diabetes is an especially serious disease.

Because it can lead to blindness, kidney failure, and a higher risk of strokes and heart attacks. Patients who develop diabetes at an early age are at greater risk. Because the effects of diabetes increase over time.

Doctors and dietitians have suggestions for parents. Who want to prevent obesity in their children. Parents encouraged, for example, not to use food as a reward for good behavior. And not to demand that children always finish everything on their plates. Parents should provide healthy snacks, like fresh fruits and vegetables. In place of junk food.

Parents can also encourage their children to exercise. By getting them involved in individual or team sports. And also limiting their television viewing to less than two hours per day.

If parents really want their children to have good diet and exercise habits. The parents should set a good example themselves. Parents can promote the health of their entire family. If they are good role models for their children.

Harcourt, Inc.

Unit Review

Identifying and Punctuating the Main Types of Sentences

Correct any run-on sentences, comma splices, or fragments in the following essay.

One of the oldest human customs is sharing a meal with other people, it is a way of showing companionship. The word *companionship* itself coming from Latin roots meaning "to share bread with someone." Because ways of eating vary from time to time and from place to place. It is interesting to compare other styles of dining with our own. The dining customs of medieval Europe are particularly interesting.

How did people dine in the castles of medieval Europe? It was customary for many people to eat together the lord of the castle had many soldiers, and he was responsible for feeding them all. The diners ate their meals in a large hall. Long wooden tables were placed along both sides of the hall these tables were for the ordinary people. The lord of the castle and his most important guests sat at a "high table." It was raised above the level of the room and was set perpendicular to the side tables. So that it could easily be seen by the other guests. The diners usually sat on benches or stools. However, the lord of the manor sat in a chair. Because he was the most important person in the room. (Even today, the leader of a meeting being called the chairperson.)

Diners in the Middle Ages did not have plates they used trenchers instead. A trencher was a large, thick slice of stale bread. Individual servings of food placed directly on the trencher. By the end of the meal, the trenchers were soaked with meat juices and sauces. After the meal was over. The trenchers were thrown to the dogs lying under the table. After large banquets, the trenchers were often collected. And given to the poor to eat.

Soups and stews were served in bowls. Two or more people sharing each bowl. In England, a portion of soup or stew was called a "mess." This is the origin of our word "mess hall." Soups and stews eaten with wooden spoons. Like the ones used for cooking today.

Spoons were usually the only utensil provided by the host diners brought their own knives to the table, and forks did not become common until the end of the sixteenth century. The first forks were used only for serving food they were large and had two prongs. Only later did people begin to use individual forks for eating. Until forks came into common use, people used their fingers to eat solid foods. The first people to use forks for eating were criticized. For being too finicky and delicate.

We may think of medieval eating habits as primitive. However, in today's modern world, "fast foods" are becoming increasingly popular. Because people want to eat in a hurry. What makes fast foods so quick and easy to eat? Are fast foods popular because we can eat so many of them with our fingers? Or because so many of them, like hot dogs, hamburgers, pizza, and tacos, are foods served on top of bread?

Harcourt, Inc.

PUNCTUATION THAT "SETS OFF" OR SEPARATES

CHAPTER 13

PARENTHETICAL EXPRESSIONS

When speaking, people often interrupt their sentences with expressions such as *by the way, after all,* or *as a matter of fact.* These expressions are not really part of the main idea of the sentence; instead, they are interrupting—or **parenthetical—** expressions. In speech, people indicate that these parenthetical expressions are not part of the main idea of the sentence by pausing and dropping their voices before and after the expression. In writing, the same pauses are indicated with commas.

You have already learned that commas may be used to separate the clauses in compound and complex sentences. Another major function of the comma is to "set off" interrupting or **parenthetical expressions** from the rest of the sentence in which they occur.

Read the following sentences aloud, and notice how the commas around the italicized parenthetical expressions correspond to the pauses you make in speech.

Harcourt, Inc.

Well, I guess I have to leave now.

She's only a child, *after all.*

Did you know, *by the way,* that we're getting a new boss?

The rule for punctuating parenthetical expressions is very simple:

A parenthetical expression must be completely set off from the rest of the sentence by commas.

This means that if the parenthetical expression occurs at the *beginning* of the sentence, it is *followed* by a comma. For example,

No, I don't know where they keep their knives.

If the parenthetical expression is at the *end* of the sentence, it is *preceded* by a comma.

He will be late again, *I suppose.*

If the parenthetical expression is in the *middle* of the sentence, it is both *preceded* and *followed* by a comma.

Some seafood, *especially swordfish and tilefish,* may contain harmful amounts of mercury.

There are many parenthetical expressions. Some of the most frequently used ones are listed below:

after all

as a matter of fact

at any rate

etc. (an abbreviation of the Latin words *et cetera,* meaning "and other things")

for example

for instance

furthermore

however

in fact

> nevertheless
>
> of course
>
> on the other hand
>
> on the whole
>
> therefore
>
> well (at the beginning of a sentence)
>
> *yes* and *no* (at the beginning of a sentence)

Expressions such as the following are often parenthetical if they occur in a position *other than* at the beginning of a sentence:

> does it
>
> doesn't it
>
> I believe
>
> I suppose
>
> I hope
>
> I think
>
> is it
>
> isn't it
>
> that is
>
> you know

For example,

> He won the election, I believe.
>
> Smoking, you know, is bad for your health.

Continual repetition of the parenthetical expression *you know* should be avoided in both speech and writing. If you are speaking clearly and your listener is paying attention, he or she knows what you are saying and does not have to be constantly reminded of the fact. Besides, you know, continually repeating *you know* can be irritating to your listener, and, you know, it doesn't really accomplish anything.

Study the following points carefully.

1. Some of the above words and phrases can be either parenthetical or not parenthetical, depending on how they are used in a sentence.

Harcourt, Inc.

If an expression is parenthetical, it can be removed from the sentence, and what remains will still be a complete sentence.

PARENTHETICAL	The problems, *after all,* are difficult.
NOT PARENTHETICAL	He left *after all* the work was done.
PARENTHETICAL	There is a football game today, *I believe.*
NOT PARENTHETICAL	*I believe* what you tell me.

2. Because the abbreviation *etc.* is parenthetical, it must be *preceded* and *followed* by a comma if it occurs in the middle of a sentence.

Books, stationary, art supplies, etc., are sold at the corner store.

The final comma after *etc.* indicates that *etc.* is parenthetical. Notice that this comma serves a different function from the commas that separate the items in the series.

3. **Conjunctive adverbs,** like *however* and *nevertheless,* are considered parenthetical and are set off from the clause in which they occur. They should be punctuated in simple sentences as follows:

I thought the plan was a secret. *However,* everyone seems to know about it.

or

I thought the plan was a secret. Everyone, *however,* seems to know about it.

In the second clause of a compound sentence, **conjunctive adverbs** should be punctuated as follows:

She earns a good salary; *nevertheless,* she always seems to be borrowing money from her friends.

The concert was long; *however,* it was quite beautiful.

The semicolon is needed because the clauses in the compound sentence are not joined by a coordinating conjunction. The semicolon also takes the place of the comma that would normally precede a parenthetical expression occurring in the middle of a sentence. A comma follows the parenthetical expression to set it off from the remainder of the sentence. (Conjunctive adverbs were discussed earlier in Lesson 9. For a complete list of them see the inside front cover of this book.)

4. People's names and titles are also set off by commas *if you are speaking directly to them* in a sentence. This type of construction is called **direct address.** The punctuation of direct address is the same as that used for parenthetical expressions.

Harcourt, Inc.

Have you played your guitar today, *Allen?*

Ladies and gentlemen, please be seated.

Notice that names and titles are set off by commas only when the person is being *directly addressed* in the sentence. Otherwise, no commas are needed.

Music has always been important to Allen. (no commas)

Allen, have you always loved music? (commas for direct address)

EXERCISE
13A

Add commas and semicolons to the following sentences wherever they are needed. If a sentence needs no additional punctuation, label it *C* for *correct*. This exercise deals only with the punctuation rules in Lesson 13.

1. All of us I believe have heard news stories about compulsive hoarders.

2. There is the elderly woman for example whose home is filled with piles of newspapers and boxes of empty bottles.

3. Many people collect certain objects however compulsive hoarders fill their homes with huge quantities of useless items.

4. Accumulated items may cover every available surface in fact there may be barely enough space to walk from one room to the next.

5. Items may be piled in stacks five or six feet high therefore walking through such a home is like traveling through tunnels of trash.

6. Danger from falling objects is a constant threat in addition a home filled with trash is also a fire hazard.

7. Piles of trash make normal housekeeping impossible for instance one hoarder had not cleaned her living room in eleven years.

8. Compulsive hoarders may be uncomfortable with their living conditions; they are nevertheless unwilling to discard any items.

9. I think one of the most extreme examples of hoarding was the case of the Collyer brothers of Manhattan.

10. In fact after the two brothers' deaths in 1941, the trash removed from their home totaled 136 tons!

11. Compulsive hoarding can be a symptom of mental illness therefore it is often treated with a combination of drugs and psychotherapy.

12. However a great deal of patience is required for instance one therapist spent twenty minutes persuading a client to discard a single box of expired coupons.

13. Therapists usually begin with a specific goal like for example clearing enough space for a client to sleep in his own bed or to eat at her own kitchen table.

14. On the whole compulsive hoarding is more common among the elderly, so with the aging of the American population, this disorder may become increasingly prevalent.

EXERCISE
13B

Add commas and semicolons to the sentences in the following essay wherever they are necessary. This exercise requires additional punctuation only for parenthetical expressions.

Shopping malls are an important feature of our commercial landscape, and it seems they increase in size with each passing year. The world's largest mall is in Edmonton, Alberta, Canada, where it covers forty-eight square city blocks and 5.2 million square feet. In fact the West Edmonton Mall is so large that its owners call it "the eighth wonder of the world."

The West Edmonton Mall has 800 shops however it is far more than just a retail center. The mall is in addition the region's main entertainment center. Its attractions include for example a roller coaster, a full-sized hockey rink, a water park, and a miniature golf course. Edmonton is the northernmost city in Canada, and in a climate as cold as Edmonton's, the mall is of course completely enclosed. This has enabled the mall to set even more world records. West Edmonton has the world's largest indoor amusement park, the largest indoor water park, and the largest indoor lagoon. The amusement park includes twenty-five rides, and the water park contains the world's largest indoor wave pool. The lagoon boasts a full-size replica of Columbus's flagship, the *Santa Maria.*

The owners of the mall, the Ghermezian family, wanted to provide Edmonton with entertainment attractions as good as, if not better than, those of full-scale amusement parks. In Disneyland for example the sub-

Harcourt, Inc.

marine ride is simulated; the vessel does not actually go below the surface of the water, and the sea life the passengers view is therefore artificial rather than real. At West Edmonton in contrast the four fully operational submarines submerge themselves below the surface of the lagoon and take their passengers on a half-hour ride past real fish shipwrecks etc. In fact the West Edmonton Mall has more submarines than the Canadian Navy! This I think is one of the most amazing facts about this remarkable mall.

It is no wonder is it that more than 20 million people from all over the world visit the West Edmonton Mall each year. And by the way because it takes more than one day to see all the mall's attractions, the mall includes its own hotel!

Harcourt, Inc.

14

APPOSITIVES

In sentences you sometimes use a noun whose meaning may not be as clear to your reader as it is to you. For example, suppose that you write:

Mr. Anderson needs to sign these forms.

If you think that your reader may not know who Mr. Anderson is, you can add a phrase to your sentence to provide more information about him.

Mr. Anderson, *the director of the Financial Aid Department,* needs to sign these forms.

This kind of explanatory phrase is called an **appositive** (from the verb to *appose,* meaning "to place things beside each other"). An appositive is a phrase placed beside a noun to clarify that noun's meaning. Study the following sentences, in which the appositives have been italicized. Notice that each appositive *immediately follows the noun it describes.*

Harcourt, Inc.

July, *the seventh month in our calendar,* was named after Julius Caesar.

The center of the farm workers' movement was Delano, *a small town north of Bakersfield, California.*

Poi, *the staple food of the Hawaiian diet,* is made from taro root.

As you can see, appositives must be set off by commas from the rest of the sentence just as parenthetical expressions are. Appositives are considered *extra* elements in a sentence because they add additional information about a noun that has already been *specifically identified.* For example, in the sentence about *July* above, even without the appositive "the seventh month in our calendar," you know which month was named after Julius Caesar because the month has been specifically identified as *July.* In the next example, even without the appositive "a small town north of Bakersfield, California," you know that the town that was the center of the farm workers' movement is *Delano.* In the third example, even without the appositive "the staple food of the Hawaiian diet," the food is specifically identified as *poi.*

Here is the rule for punctuating this kind of explanatory phrase or clause:

If a phrase or clause adds additional information about a noun that has already been specifically identified, that phrase or clause must be completely set off from the rest of the sentence by commas.

In this lesson, you will be dealing with appositives, which are phrases. In Lesson 15, you will be applying the same rule to clauses.

Specifically identified includes mentioning either a person's first or last name, or both, or using words such as "my oldest brother," "my ten o'clock class on Monday," or "my hometown." The nouns in the last three phrases are considered to be *specifically identified* because even though you have not mentioned your brother's name, you can have only one "oldest" brother. Similarly, only one specific class can be your "ten o'clock class on Monday," and only one specific town can be your "hometown." In other words, *specifically identified* means limiting the meaning of a general word like *town* to *one particular town* or limiting a general word like *class* to *one particular class.*

Underline the appositives in the following sentences, and then punctuate them. Remember that appositives *follow* the nouns that they describe.

My oldest brother a doctor at Queen of Angels Hospital is attending a medical convention in San Francisco.

My twelve o'clock class on Tuesday English 110 concentrates on writing.

This summer I'm going to visit my hometown Salinas, California.

Boston, Massachusetts the home of many universities is my favorite city to visit.

Each spring I return to San Francisco the city of hills and cable cars.

Harcourt, Inc.

On the other hand, if a phrase is *necessary* to establish the specific identity of a noun, it is *not set off* by commas. Study the difference between the following pair of sentences.

The novel *Great Expectations* is considered by many critics to be Charles Dickens's greatest work. (No commas are used to set off *Great Expectations* because the title is necessary to identify which of Dickens's many novels is considered to be his greatest work.)

Charles Dickens's fourteenth novel, *Great Expectations,* is considered by many critics to be his greatest work. (Commas are used to set off *Great Expectations* because Dickens's greatest work has already been specifically identified as his *fourteenth* novel.)

Most single-word appositives are necessary to establish the specific identity of the nouns they follow and are therefore *not* set off by commas.

The color *yellow* is my favorite.

My sister *Susan* lives in Detroit.

The word *penurious* means "stingy."

Underline the appositives in the following sentences, and then add commas wherever they are necessary. Some sentences may not require commas.

Fiat automobiles are manufactured in Turin a city in northeastern Italy.

The komodor a Hungarian sheepdog has a coat that looks like a mop.

Balboa a sixteenth-century Spanish explorer was the first European to discover the American side of the Pacific Ocean.

In Europe, fruits and vegetables are usually sold by the kilogram an amount equal to 2.2 pounds.

My older brother an orthopedic surgeon spends much of his time working on injured athletes.

Have you seen the movie *Titanic?*

EXERCISE
14A

Add commas to the following sentences wherever they are necessary. If a sentence needs no additional punctuation, label it *C* for *correct*. This exercise covers only the rules from Lesson 14.

1. New Mexico "the birthplace of the Nuclear Age" also contains many early historical sites.

2. The Native American village of Acoma the oldest continuously occupied site in the United States has been inhabited since A.D. 1150.

3. Acoma sits on a high mesa an elevated plateau 350 feet above sea level.

4. Throughout the state, you can see ancient Indian cliff dwellings built with adobe sun-dried bricks made of clay and straw.

5. Santa Fe the state capital has New Mexico's typical mixture of Native American, Spanish, and Anglo cultures.

6. The town is built around the Spanish Mission of San Miguel one of the nation's oldest churches.

7. The Institute of American Indian Art one of more than thirty Indian tribal colleges attracts students from all over the United States.

8. Each year, opera buffs flock to the Santa Fe Opera an unusual open-air operatic venue.

9. Taos a center of art and tourism is famous for both its fine art galleries and shops and for its ski resorts.

10. Fort Sumner a nineteenth-century army post and Indian reservation recalls a sad event in the state's history.

11. In 1864, more than 8,000 Navajos were forced to make the Long Walk a 400-mile forced march from Arizona to their new reservation at Fort Sumner.

12. The Nuclear Age began in the town of Los Alamos the site of World War II's Manhattan Project.

13. This top-secret project built Little Boy and Fat Man the two atomic bombs dropped over Japan in 1945.

14. Natural attractions include beautiful national forests and the famous limestone formations of Carlsbad Caverns one of the world's largest cave systems.

15. With its wide variety of scenic, artistic, and historical sites, New Mexico lives up to its state motto "The Land of Enchantment."

EXERCISE
14B

Add commas and semicolons to the following sentences wherever they are necessary. If a sentence needs no additional punctuation, label it *C* for *correct*. This exercise covers punctuation rules from Lessons 13 and 14.

1. Almost everyone has had some kind of contact with the ancient study of astrology.

2. Today people distinguish between astrology the art of divination and astronomy the science of the stars.

3. However up through the Middle Ages, these two studies were indistinguishable, and in fact astrology was understood to be part of the Classical tradition the learning we associate with ancient Greece and Rome.

4. Originating in ancient Mesopotamia around the third millennium B.C., it reached its fullest Western world height during the Hellenistic period of Greece the time of philosophers like Ptolemy and Epicurus.

5. People habitually used horoscopes predictive readings obtained by special mappings of the stars when a new child was born or at the beginning of a marriage.

6. Christianity later challenged the use of astrology because it asserted that the astrology left little room for free will one of the critical qualities that distinguishes humans from other living creatures.

7. Yet even at the heart of Christianity, there is evidence of astrology in the story of the Magi the three wise men led by a star to the Nativity.

8. Astrology remained important until Copernicus a Renaissance astronomer showed that the sun, and not the Earth, was the center of the universe.

9. Today, astrology is not considered to be a science nevertheless people all over the world still believe in it.

10. You can find horoscopes in the daily newspaper, in magazines, and in many sites on the World Wide Web the high-tech soothsayer of our times!

11. We are of course all familiar with the twelve different "signs" that correspond with both the constellations and the months of the year.

12. Each constellation has an animal or mythic figure which it is named for; "Leo" for example covers the period from July 23 to August 22 and is represented by the lion.

13. The characteristics of the lion pride and courage are said to be found in those people who fall under this sign.

14. The signs are also divided into the categories of water, air, earth, and fire the four elements of life on earth.

15. Because Leo is a fire sign, Leos of course are supposed to be fiery people too!

16. Whether or not you actually believe in the predictive accuracy of astrology, you read your horoscope at least once in a while don't you?

Harcourt, Inc.

CHAPTER 15

RESTRICTIVE AND NONRESTRICTIVE CLAUSES

In Lesson 14 you learned that if a phrase adds extra information about a noun that has already been specifically identified, that phrase (an **appositive**) must be set off by commas. For example,

Many of NBC's television shows are filmed in Burbank, *a city in the San Fernando Valley.*

The appositive is set off by commas because the place in which many of NBC's television shows are filmed has already been specifically identified as *Burbank*.

On the other hand, if a phrase is necessary to establish the specific identity of a noun, the phrase is *not* set off by commas.

The verb *to be* is the most irregular verb in the English language.

The phrase *to be* is not set off by commas because it is necessary to identify which specific verb is the most irregular verb in the English language.

The same rule that applies to the punctuation of appositive phrases also applies to the punctuation of *clauses.* Read the following sentences, in which the dependent clauses have been italicized. Can you see why one sentence in each pair has commas while the other does not?

The woman *whom you have just met* is in charge of the program.

Teresa Gomez, *whom you have just met,* is in charge of the program.

The book *which I am now reading* is an anthology of African American literature.

Black Voices, which I am now reading, is an anthology of African American literature.

In the first sentence of each pair, the dependent clause is necessary to establish the specific identity of the noun it follows. This type of clause is called a **restrictive** clause because it *restricts,* or limits, the meaning of the word it describes. For example, in the first sentence if the restrictive clause were removed, the sentence would read:

The woman is in charge of the program.

The meaning of this sentence is unclear because there are billions of women in the world, and any one of them might be in charge of the program. But when the clause is added to the sentence, the meaning of the general word *woman* is now restricted, or limited, to *one particular woman—the woman whom you have just met.* Thus, the restrictive clause "whom you have just met" establishes the specific identity of the word *woman.*

Similarly, in the third sentence above, the clause "which I am now reading" identifies *which* book is in an anthology of African American literature. It restricts the general word *book* to *one particular book—the book which I am now reading.*

Because restrictive clauses are necessary to establish the specific identity of the nouns they describe, the following punctuation rule applies:

Restrictive clauses are not set off by commas.

In contrast, the clauses in the second and fourth sentences are *not* necessary to identify which particular woman is in charge of the program or which particular book is an anthology of African American literature. In these sentences, the woman has already been identified as *Teresa Gomez,* and the book has already been identified as *Black Voices.* Because these clauses are *not* restrictive clauses, they are called **nonrestrictive clauses.** Nonrestrictive clauses merely add extra information about the nouns they describe. They serve the same function as appositives and are punctuated in the same way.

Nonrestrictive clauses must be completely set off from by the rest of the sentence commas.

This means that if a nonrestrictive clause is at the *end* of a sentence, it will be *preceded* by a comma. If it is in the *middle* of a sentence, it will be *both preceded and followed* by a comma. (Like appositives, nonrestrictive clauses never occur at the beginning of a sentence because they must follow the noun that they describe.)

The restrictive and nonrestrictive clauses that you have been studying are called adjective clauses because, like adjectives, these clauses describe nouns. The words that most frequently introduce adjective clauses are:

that

where

which

who

whom

whose

Like all clauses, adjective clauses must contain both a subject and a verb. But notice that in adjective clauses *the word that introduces the clause may also be the subject of the clause.*

          S   V
The house *which once occupied this lot* was destroyed by fire.

Or the clause may contain a separate subject:

        S V
The wallet *that I lost* contained all my credit cards.

Adjective clauses, like adverb clauses, are used in **complex sentences.** Although these sentences may not seem to be complex at first glance, if you study the sentences above, you will see that each of them has two subjects and two verbs. Also, if the adjective clause, which is the **dependent clause,** is removed from the sentence, a complete independent clause remains.

	S V
INDEPENDENT CLAUSE	The house was destroyed by fire.

	S V
DEPENDENT CLAUSE	which once occupied this lot

	S V
INDEPENDENT CLAUSE	The wallet contained all my credit cards.
	S V
DEPENDENT CLAUSE	that I lost

An adjective clause often occurs in the middle of a sentence because it must follow the noun it describes. When an adjective clause is in the middle of a sentence, part of the independent clause precedes it, and the rest of the independent clause follows it. For example,

> S   V
> Food *which is high in calories* often tastes better than low-calorie food.

> S   V
> The National Museum of the American Indian, *which currently is located in New York City,* will move to Washington, D.C., in 2003.

A sentence may contain more than one adjective clause. Each clause is punctuated separately. In the following sentences, the first adjective clause is *nonrestrictive* (with commas), and the second clause is *restrictive* (no commas).

> The San Fernando Valley, *which suffered a large earthquake in 1994,* has since experienced aftershocks *that distress many people.*

> The Cadillac automobile, *which was originally manufactured in Detroit,* is named after the French explorer *who founded the city.*

Underline every adjective clause in each of the following sentences, and circle the noun it describes. Then decide which clauses are restrictive (and do *not* need commas) and which clauses are nonrestrictive (and *do* need commas). Add the appropriate punctuation.

Note: Although clauses beginning with *who, whom, whose, where,* or *which* may be either restrictive or nonrestrictive, clauses that begin with *that* are *always* restrictive.

> Union Square which is one of San Francisco's main shopping areas is known for its open-air flower stalls.

> The classes that I am taking this semester are all easy for me.

> Most tourists who come to Los Angeles also visit Disneyland which is less than an hour's drive from the city.

Harcourt, Inc.

The candidate whom we supported was not elected.

Ms. Gomez whose native language is Spanish also speaks French, German, and English.

He is an artist whom we all admire a great deal.

EXERCISE
15A

Each of the following sentences contains one or more adjective clauses. Underline each adjective clause, and circle the noun or pronouns it describes. If the clause is nonrestrictive and needs additional punctuation, add a comma or commas wherever necessary. If all of the adjective clauses in a sentence are restrictive and the sentence needs no additional punctuation, label it C for *correct*.

1. Among the many foods that Native Americans gave to the world is the chile pepper.

2. Chiles were named "peppers" by Christopher Columbus who mistakenly thought they were related to black pepper.

3. Actually, chiles are part of the Solanaceae or nightshade family which also includes tomatoes, eggplants, and potatoes.

4. The essential ingredient in chiles is capsaicin, a chemical compound that gives the peppers their hot taste.

5. A chile's heat is measured by the Scoville Scale which ranges from 0 for bell peppers to 5,000 for jalapeños which are a common ingredient in Mexican cooking.

6. This scale is named for Wilbur Scoville who first developed a standard for measuring capsaicin's power.

7. Habaneros which are the hottest of all chiles have a Scoville rating of 200,000!

8. In the past, chiles were used in ways that seem unusual to modern cooks.

9. For example, Moctezuma who was the last Aztec emperor drank a beverage made from chocolate and chiles for breakfast.

10. Today, one of the best known uses for chiles is Tabasco sauce which appears on restaurant tables throughout the Southwest as routinely as salt and pepper.

11. Other chile products that can be found in the Southwest include jalapeño jelly, chile-flavored potato chips, and even habanero lollipops.

12. If you want to sample foods that use a lot of chiles, go to any restaurant that serves Mexican, Szechuan Chinese, or East Indian food.

13. In fact, the growing popularity of chile peppers in the United States is probably due to increased immigration from parts of the world where these peppers play an important role in the native cuisine.

14. Capsaicin also has chemical properties that enable it to be used for purposes other than food.

15. Because one of these chemicals tends to numb pain, capsaicin is made into an ointment that is used to treat aching muscles.

16. The pepper sprays that police officers use to subdue criminals also contain capsaicin which is a powerful irritant to the eyes and the respiratory system.

17. Most of the information for this exercise was taken from an article titled "Care for a Little Hellish Relish?" which appeared in the January 1992 edition of the *Smithsonian* magazine.

18. The article's author who sampled habaneros as part of his research was James Robbins.

EXERCISE
15B

Add commas and semicolons to the essay below wherever necessary. This exercise covers the punctuation rules in Lessons 13–15.

Most of us I think are thrilled to have lots of choices in life, and today's supermarkets offer us an amazing array of possibilities. Therefore it's difficult to imagine a grocery store that offered only a handful of choices isn't it? However as a small child, I often visited such a store. It was run by two very kind people Mr. and Mrs. Green who lived upstairs from their store. My mother would often send me down the street to Green's Grocery which was very small and had only three aisles.

I guess I always felt safe when I entered their place. I would bring a list that my mother had written and give it to Mrs. Green who was always standing behind the counter. My mother usually wanted me to buy bread and milk which were two items we would run out of a lot. The Greens would talk to me and sometimes accompany me up and down the aisles until I found the items that my mother wanted. Usually, I'd see just a couple of different kinds of bread. Wonder Bread which was a sponsor of many children's television programs seemed to be the biggest seller. It's hard to believe, but only one brand of milk Carnation was available in their refrigerator section. I'd give the Greens my money which I'd held tightly in my hand until then and then we'd wave good-bye. Sometimes I'd forget the money or not have enough. Believe it or not Mr. Green who was in charge of the cash register would just say, "Pay me the next time!"

Today of course our markets are very different places. First of all there are dozens of different varieties of the same item. White bread for instance comes in varieties like buttermilk, potato, and Dutch dill. Furthermore different companies make different versions of the same item. My supermarket offers sourdough bread from three different bakeries. Even pet food comes in a wide variety of flavors so that owners can choose the flavor that most appeals to their pet. Is a cat who eats liver paté any better than one who eats plain tuna? Purina which is a major pet food manufacturer even offers special formulas for pets that are aging or that are overweight!

I guess the simpler world of Green's Grocery is gone, as are the people who ran it. I recently saw a commercial on television aimed at viewers who find even a supermarket's choices too limiting. Now it is possible to order cereals which you can design yourself to contain any ingredients that you want. They are available on the World Wide Web which is our newest shopping venue for $8 a box, plus shipping.

Are you the kind of person who would be interested in such a product?

Harcourt, Inc.

16

ITEMS IN A SERIES AND DATES AND ADDRESSES

A series consists of *three or more* related items. Commas are placed between each item in a series.

Danish, Swedish, and *Norwegian* are related languages.

For dessert you may choose *ice cream, sherbet,* or *tapioca.*

To qualify for this job, you must have *a master's degree in international relations, at least three years of work experience,* and the ability to *speak both Spanish and Portuguese.*

Although some writers consider the final comma before the conjunction (*and, or,* or *nor*) optional, using it is preferred, especially in formal writing.

However, if *every* item in a series is joined by a conjunction, no commas are needed because the conjunctions keep the individual items separated. This type of construction is used only when the writer wishes to place particular emphasis on the number of items in the series.

The backyard of this house has *a swimming pool* and *a Jacuzzi* and *a hot tub.*

If a date or an address consists of more than one item, a comma is used after *each* part of the date or the address, *including a comma after the last item.* (If the last item in the series is also the last word in the sentence, only a period follows it.) Notice that this punctuation rule differs from the rule used for punctuating an ordinary series.

My grandparents will celebrate their fiftieth wedding anniversary on October 11, 1999, with a party for all of their family.

The name of the month and the number of the day (October 11) are considered a single item and are separated from the year by a comma. However, notice that a comma also *follows* 1999, which is the last item in the date.

We moved from Norman, Oklahoma, to Flagstaff, Arizona, in 1995.

Notice the commas after "Oklahoma" and "Arizona." These commas are used in addition to the commas that separate the names of the cities from the names of the states.

If a date or an address consists of only a single item, no comma is necessary.

December 25 is Christmas.

We moved from Oklahoma to Arizona.

A comma is not used before a ZIP code number.

The mailing address for Hollywood is Los Angeles, California 90028.

Punctuate the following sentences.

The armistice signed on November 11 1918 ended the fighting in World War I.

Because of the multicultural character of my neighborhood, church bazaars sell tacos pizza teriyaki chow mein and hot dogs.

The coffee shop's special club sandwich contains ham and cheese and turkey.

I can't believe that you drove from Portland Oregon to Newark New Jersey in three days.

John F. Kennedy Aldous Huxley and C. S. Lewis all died on November 22 1963.

Harcourt, Inc.

EXERCISE
16A

Add commas to the following sentences wherever needed. If a sentence needs no additional commas, label it *C* for *correct*. This exercise covers only the punctuation rules from Lesson 16.

1. The last major battle of the American Revolution ended on October 19 1781 in Yorktown Virginia when British general Charles Cornwallis surrendered to George Washington.

2. This war involved American British and French troops.

3. The oldest Jewish house of worship in the United States is the Touro Synagogue at 1585 Touro Street Newport Rhode Island.

4. Roger Williams Park in Providence Rhode Island is named after the state's founder and includes a natural history museum a planetarium and a zoo.

5. It takes a day to travel by car between Kingman Arizona and Malibu California.

6. The French dish called *cassoulet* is a treat for meat lovers, for it contains not only pork but also lamb and duck and sausage.

7. Your term paper must be turned in by May 15 2002.

8. Sue was born on January 1 2001 and abbreviates her birth date as 01-01-01.

9. I have read the English Romantic poets Wordsworth and Coleridge but not Byron Keats or Shelley.

10. The town of Lowell Massachusetts was a center of the United States' textile industry during the nineteenth century.

11. The legacy of this industry is preserved in the city's American Textile History Museum the Boott Cotton Mills Museum and Lowell National Historical Park.

12. August 14 is my parents' fortieth wedding anniversary, and we will have a party for them at the Terrace Inn at 965 East Lake Avenue Burlingame Vermont.

13. To apply for this job, you must show a résumé proof of legal residence and three letters of recommendation.

14. Your blind date has good looks and money and charm, so what are you worried about?

15. Who cares if he also has an ex-wife three small children and a few debts?

EXERCISE
16B

Add semicolons and commas wherever necessary in the following essay. This exercise covers all the lessons on punctuation in Unit Four.

Some highly experienced travelers say that the best way to see any country is to walk through it. Of course walking through a relatively small country is a much more practical proposition than walking through a large one. Walking also requires the right equipment. Hiking shoes and rain gear and a good hat are all crucial. A sturdy backpack sunglasses and a water bottle are also required. When you walk, you must carry much of your world with you.

The best way to understand the virtues of a walking tour is to learn about a particular one. William O' Reilly a professor from a college in Southern California led a walking tour of western Ireland in August 1992. The group consisted of Professor O'Reilly eight students who had taken his British literature course and Mrs. O'Reilly who is a geology instructor at the same college. The group completed a four-week walking tour of the Dingle Peninsula County Kerry and the Cliff of Moher.

The group landed at Shannon Airport on Monday August 3 and gathered in the city of Limerick in County Limerick. From there, they took buses trains and taxis to the smaller city of Tralee in County Kerry. Their walk on the Dingle Peninsula began on Tuesday August 4. After they crossed a low mountain range, they proceeded along a two-lane highway to the town of Dingle which is the center of commerce industry and culture for this area. In the pubs of Dingle, the O'Reillys and the students and the locals all sang Irish folk songs until closing time. Then the college group headed west toward Slea Head one of the westernmost pieces of land in Europe. There they marveled at the raw beauty of a place where the sea sky and mountains all meet in a spectacular symphony.

Next, the group walked out of Ennistymon and along the Cliffs of Moher which are an extraordinary formation of cliffs that rise 700 feet straight out of the sea. They hiked paused to gape and stopped to eat along those rugged cliffs. It was only after they had completed a long walk along the edge of the cliffs that they noticed a huge sign which warned hikers from doing what they had just done! The sign had been placed at the wrong end of the walk! The group was amazed scared relieved and excited that they had successfully completed such a dangerous hike.

This was the end of the first half of their trip. From this account, you can see that walking is hard and tiring but also exhilarating. On August 30 they completed the second leg of their walk and then flew back to Newark New Jersey where they caught a connecting flight to Los Angeles. After arriving in Los Angeles, the students went home, but the O'Reillys caught still another flight to Seattle Washington to spend a week relaxing with their oldest son who works for Boeing Aircraft there.

Harcourt, Inc.

Unit Review

Punctuation That "Sets Off" or Separates

Add commas and semicolons to the following essay wherever necessary.

A plant that is considered valuable in one country can be a pest in another. A good example of this phenomenon is the vine which is known as *kuzu* in Japan and "kudzu" in the United States.

In Japan which is its native country kudzu is a highly prized wild plant that grows mainly in mountainous regions. Its leaves vine shoots flowers and roots are all put to use; none of the plant is wasted.

In the United States on the other hand kudzu is often regarded as a nuisance. Kudzu was first brought to the United States in 1876, and it now grows throughout the South. In fact the main objection which many Southerners have to kudzu is its amazing ability to grow. The South's climate is much more favorable to kudzu than Japan's, and most Japanese would be astonished by the growth rate of American kudzu. For example under ideal conditions, kudzu can grow one foot a day or up to 100 feet in a single season. In addition, when kudzu runs out of room to grow on the ground, it starts to grow skyward. Kudzu destroys valuable timber by climbing up trees and smothering them with its dense foliage. It even climbs power poles and shorts out transmission lines. Worst of all however is its sneaky habit of invading farmland and destroying crops. James Dickey a noted Southern writer has gone so far as to call kudzu "a vegetable form of cancer."

Because kudzu is a wild plant, it grows without fertilizer irrigation or any care at all. In fact one of the South's most difficult problems is to find a way to kill kudzu. Only the most toxic herbicides can destroy kudzu; however these chemicals leave the land unfit for growing other crops. Many people resort to seemingly endless attempts to chop down dig up plow under and burn kudzu.

Is there a solution to the kudzu problem? Well in Japan powdered kudzu roots are used in traditional herbal medicines and in foods like kudzu noodles kudzu tea kudzu gelatin and kudzu candy. Its leaves shoots and flowers are eaten as vegetables. Kudzu vines are used to make rope and to weave textiles furthermore kudzu can also be used for hay and silage. Perhaps the United States could also learn to process kudzu into useful products which could help turn a pest into a profitable crop.

An excellent book which describes the many uses of kudzu is *The Book of Kudzu* by William Shurtleff and Akiko Aoyagi. It is published by Autumn Press at 7 Littell Road Brookline Massachusetts 02146, but the book is I believe no longer in print.

Harcourt, Inc.

UNIT 5

PRONOUN USAGE

CHAPTER 17

SUBJECT, OBJECT, AND POSSESSIVE PRONOUNS

Pronouns are words that are used to refer to persons, places, things, and ideas without repeating their names. In other words, pronouns are used in place of nouns. For example, rather than saying "Ben lost Ben's notebook last night, but Ben found the notebook this morning," you can say, "Ben lost *his* notebook last night, but *he* found *it* this morning." In this sentence, the pronoun *his* replaces *Ben's*, the pronoun *he* replaces *Ben*, and the pronoun *it* replaces *notebook*. The noun that the pronoun replaces is called the **antecedent** (Latin for "to go before") of the pronoun.

There are several different kinds of pronouns, but in this lesson you will be studying only **subject pronouns, object pronouns,** and **possessive pronouns.**

Singular Pronouns

Subject	*Object*	*Possessive*
I	me	my, mine
you	you	your, yours

Harcourt, Inc.

Subject	Object	Possessive
he	him	his
she	her	her, hers
it	it	its

Plural Pronouns

Subject	Object	Possessive
we	us	our, ours
you	you	your, yours
they	them	their, theirs

As their name suggests, **subject pronouns** are used as the *subject* of a sentence or a clause. For example,

He is a good dancer.

We went to the park together.

In *formal* speech and writing, subject pronouns are also used after forms of the verb *be,* as in:

That is *she* singing with the chorus.

It is *I.*

If I were *she,* I'd have come to the lecture.

In formal speech and writing, subject pronouns are used after forms of the verb *be* because they refer to the *same* thing or person as the subject.

That = she singing with the chorus.

It = I.

I = she

However, in *informal* speech, many people would use object pronouns in the sentences below.

That is (or That's) *her* singing with the chorus.

It is (or It's) *me.*

If I were *her,* I'd have come to the lecture.

Harcourt, Inc.

Whether you choose to say "it is I" or "it is me" depends on the circumstances. If you are taking an English test or writing a formal essay, using subject pronouns after forms of *be* is appropriate and expected. But if you are speaking casually with a friend, "It is I" may sound artificial, and the informal "It is me" might be more suitable.

In this unit, you will be studying both grammar and usage. Try to keep clear in your mind those situations in which you have a choice between formal and informal constructions (usage) and those situations in which only one pronoun form is correct at all times (grammar).

"It is *we*" versus "It is *us*" = usage.

"Al and *I* are here" versus "Al and *me* are here" = grammar.

Object pronouns are used as objects of prepositions, as direct objects, and as indirect objects.

You will remember that the noun or pronoun in a prepositional phrase is called the **object of the preposition.** That is why an object pronoun replaces the noun. For example,

The award was given to *Matthew*.

The award was given to *him*.

Please sit by *Cathy*.

Please sit by *her*.

Object pronouns are also used as direct objects. A **direct object** is the word that *receives* the action of the verb and, with very few exceptions, follows the verb, often as the next word.

     S   DO
The artist painted that *picture*.

The artist painted *it*.

  S   DO
He composed that *song* last night.

He composed *it* last night.

Another way that object pronouns are used is as indirect objects. An **indirect object** is the person or thing *to whom* or *for whom* something is done.

  S   IO   DO
She made *Robert* a chocolate cake.

She made *him* a chocolate cake.

The previous sentence is another way of saying, "She made a chocolate cake *for him.*"

> ```
>        S              IO   DO
> ```
> Benjamin gave his sister a gift.
>
> Benjamin gave *her* a gift.

The previous sentence is another way of saying, "Benjamin gave a gift *to her.*"

Possessive pronouns are used to show ownership.

> The cat scratched *its* neck.
>
> The children stamped *their* feet in joy.

Very few people make pronoun errors when there is only one subject or one object in a sentence. For example, no native speaker of English would say, "Us is here" instead of "We are here." However, people often do make mistakes when two subjects or two objects are paired up in a sentence. For example, which of the following two sentences is grammatically correct?

> Barbara bought Kevin and *me* some good cookies.
>
> Barbara bought Kevin and *I* some good cookies.

To determine the correct pronoun in this kind of "double" construction, split the sentence in two like this:

1. Barbara bought Kevin some good cookies.
2. Barbara bought (me, I) some good cookies.

As you can tell after you have split the sentence in two, it would be incorrect to say "Barbara bought *I* some good cookies." The correct pronoun is *me,* which is the indirect object of the verb *gave.* Therefore, the whole sentence should read:

> Barbara bought Kevin and *me* some good cookies.
>
> Which of the following two sentences is correct?

> The mayor congratulated Rick and *I.*
>
> The mayor congratulated Rick and *me.*

> Again, split the sentences in two.

1. The mayor congratulated Rick.
2. The mayor congratulated (me, I).

Harcourt, Inc.

Now, which pronoun is correct?

Another very common pronoun error is using subject pronouns instead of object pronouns after prepositions. The object of a preposition must be an *object* pronoun. Which of the following two sentences is correct?

The teacher handed new books to Sam and *I.*

The teacher handed new books to Sam and *me.*

If you split the sentence in two, you have:

1. The teacher handed new books to Sam.
2. The teacher handed new books to (me, I).

The correct pronoun is *me,* which is the object of the preposition *to.* Therefore, the correct sentence is:

The teacher handed new books to Sam and *me.*

It is extremely important that you do not decide which pronoun to use simply on the basis of what "sounds better" *unless you split the sentence in two first.* To many people, "The teacher handed new books to Sam and I" sounds "more correct" than "The teacher handed new books to Sam and *me,*" yet, as you have seen, *me* is actually the correct pronoun.

Another example of choosing an incorrect pronoun because it "sounds better" is the frequent misuse of the subject pronoun *I* after the preposition *between.* As you already know, the object of a preposition must be an *object* pronoun. Therefore, it is always incorrect to say "between you and *I.*" The correct construction is "between you and *me.*"

Circle the pronoun that correctly completes each of the following sentences.

Between you and (I, me), that's a wonderful movie.

The teacher rewarded Joseph and (I, me) for our presentation.

Ken and (she, her) speak frequently.

Helene made Sasha and (I, me) Halloween costumes.

The party was for their class and (we, us).

Occasionally you may use constructions like the following:

We freshmen must pre-enroll for our classes.

Most of *us nurses* would prefer to work the 7 A.M. to 3 P.M. shift.

Harcourt, Inc.

To determine whether the sentence requires a subject or an object pronoun, see which pronoun would be correct if the pronoun appeared in the sentence by itself rather than being followed by a noun.

(We, us) citizens should vote in each election.

(We, us) should vote in each election.

Give a raise to (we, us) good workers.

Give a raise to (we, us).

The correct pronouns are *we* citizens and *us* workers.

Circle the pronoun that correctly completes each of the following sentences.

Some theaters give a discount to (we, us) students.

Actors depend on the support of (we, us) fans.

(We, us) customers want the store to stay open later.

Harcourt, Inc.

EXERCISE
17A

The first part of this exercise is intended for a quick review of subject and object pronouns. Reverse each sentence so that the subject pronoun becomes the object and the object pronoun becomes the subject.

> Example: *I* saw *them* at the play.
> Answer: *They* saw *me* at the play.

1. *I* explained the lesson to *her.*

2. *He* should phone *you* tonight.

3. *We* are giving a surprise party for *them.*

4. *She* will help *us* plan the party.

5. *They* have known *me* for ten years.

6. *You* need to see *him* as soon as possible.

Circle the pronoun that correctly completes each sentence. Remember to split the sentence first if it contains a "double" construction. Apply the rules of formal English usage.

7. My neighbors invited my husband and (I, me) to their son's wedding.

8. It is (she, her) who has the information you need.

9. (We, us) taxpayers should know what the government is doing with our money.

10. He's trying to keep you and (I, me) from knowing what he's doing.

11. Can you come to the football game with your sons and (we, us)?

12. If I were (he, him), I'd pay my bills on time.

13. It's time for all of (we, us) parents to demand better schools.

14. The doctor told her brother and (she, her) that their mother needed immediate surgery.

15. (We, us) investors need reliable financial information.

16. This is a problem that concerns only (they, them) and their children.

17. The barking dog kept our neighbors and (we, us) awake all night.

18. This decision should be made by you and (she, her).

19. Tell Sam and (I, me) when the next meeting will be.

20. This agreement was a secret between (she, her) and her boss.

Harcourt, Inc.

EXERCISE
17B

Some of the following sentences contain pronoun errors. Cross out the incorrect pronouns, and write in the correct forms. If a sentence contains no pronoun errors, label it C for *correct*. Apply the rules of formal English usage.

1. Us citizens have a duty to vote each and every election.

2. The reporter questioned John and I.

3. If you buy the tickets for Kevin and I, we will make dinner.

4. She passed the torch of hope to we athletes.

5. Between you and me, I love old movies!

6. Him and Julia have been dating for about a year.

7. Ben and he play video games for hours.

8. Did you write that music for the class and I?

9. The team gave we coaches a wonderful surprise dinner.

10. It was she who won the competition.

11. The theater piece made her and I laugh a whole lot last night.

12. Will you play that new song you wrote for us students?

13. Neither Julia nor him was worried about their final exams.

14. We graduating students offer you our best wishes.

15. He worked very hard on that assignment, and between you and I, he should have received a higher grade.

16. Someone sold Bill and I fake tickets to the concert.

17. Whenever we see Sasha and him, they are laughing.

18. Rachel surprised we children with a dog named Rascal.

19. Joe and me worked hard to clean the house for the party.

Harcourt, Inc.

CHAPTER 18

PRONOUNS IN COMPARISONS AND PRONOUNS WITH *-SELF, -SELVES*

USING PRONOUNS IN COMPARISONS

In speech and in writing, we often compare two people or two things with each other. For example,

> Rose is older than I am.
>
> The company pays *Ellen* a higher salary than it pays *me*.

In the sentences above, it is easy to tell whether a subject pronoun or an object pronoun should be used in each comparison. In the first sentence, the subject pronoun *I* is correct because it would be clearly ungrammatical to say "Rose is older than *me* am." In the second sentence, the object pronoun *me* is correct because you would not say that "The company pays Ellen a higher salary than it pays *I*."

However, people usually do not write out their comparisons completely. They use a shortened form instead. For example,

> Mary Anne plays tennis better than *I*.
>
> The accident injured Sam more than *me*.

In these cases, it is possible to determine which pronoun is correct by mentally filling in the words that have been left out of the comparison.

Harcourt, Inc.

Mary Anne plays tennis better than I (do).

The accident injured Sam more than (it injured) me.

Fill in the missing words to determine which pronouns are correct in the following sentences.

Clarence can run longer distances than (I, me).

I enjoy classical music more than (he, him).

This trip will be more interesting for you than (she, her).

That dress looks better on you than (she, her).

Doing sit-ups is easier for you than (I, me).

When you fill in the missing words, the correct comparisons are

Clarence can run longer distances than *I* (can).

I enjoy classical music more than *he* (does).

This trip will be more interesting for you than (it will be for) *her.*

That dress looks better on you than (it does on) *her.*

Doing sit-ups is easier for you than (it is for) *me.*

In *informal* usage, you often hear people use object pronouns instead of subject pronouns in comparisons (for example, "He's taller than me" instead of "He's taller than I"). However, these forms are generally considered inappropriate in writing and formal speech. You should be especially careful in situations where the wrong pronoun can change the meaning of the entire sentence. For example, "Mary danced with George more than *I* (danced with him)" does not mean the same thing as "Mary danced with George more than (she danced with) *me.*" In addition, using the wrong pronoun can sometimes lead to unintentionally ridiculous sentences, like the following:

My husband likes sports more than me.

Unless the husband happens to like sports more than he likes his wife, the correct pronoun would be:

My husband likes sports more than *I* (do).

(Note: The conjunction *than,* which is used in comparisons, should not be confused with the adverb *then.*)

Avoiding Doubled Subjects

Do not "double," or repeat, the subject of a sentence by repeating the noun in its pronoun form.

INCORRECT	My sister, she is a nurse.
CORRECT	My sister is a nurse.
INCORRECT	The Johnsons, they are our neighbors.
CORRECT	The Johnsons are our neighbors.

Pronouns with *-self, -selves*

Some pronouns end in *-self* or *-selves:*

Singular	*Plural*
myself	ourselves
yourself	yourselves
himself	themselves
herself	
itself	

These pronouns can be used in two ways. They can be **reflexive pronouns.** Reflexive pronouns are used when the object of the verb or the object of the preposition is the same person or thing as the subject. For example,

I cut *myself*. (myself = I)

They will do the job by *themselves*. (themselves = they)

The family enjoyed *themselves* at the party. (themselves = relatives)

Or they may be used for *emphasis.*

Frank *himself* admits that he is lazy.

Her husband is a famous composer, and she *herself* is a well-known singer.

We *ourselves* are responsible for our decisions.

Harcourt, Inc.

Notice that the singular forms of reflexive pronouns end in *-self,* and the plural forms end in *-selves.* In standard English, there are no such forms as *hisself, ourselfs, theirselfs,* or *themselfs.* These forms are considered nonstandard in both speech and writing and should be avoided unless you are using a dialect, such as you might do in writing a story.

In formal English, the reflexive pronoun *myself* is not used in place of a subject or an object pronoun.

INCORRECT	John and myself are going out.
CORRECT	John and I are going out.
INCORRECT	The director asked Carol and myself to read the script.
CORRECT	The director asked Carol and me to read the script.

Myself is sometimes used as a subject or an object pronoun in informal usage, but even in these cases the use of the correct subject or object pronoun is preferred. Referring to yourself as *myself* rather than as *I* or *me* does *not* make you sound more polite or more modest.

EXERCISE
18A

Part One: Circle the pronoun that most logically and correctly completes each sentence. Apply the rules of formal English usage. This exercise covers only the rules in Lesson 18.

1. Nobody knows more about this project than (I, me).

2. We should do all the work (ourselfs, ourselves).

3. I thought I deserved a raise more than (he, him).

4. They made all the party decorations (theirselves, themselves).

5. Either my partner or (I, me, myself) will close this deal.

6. They have worked here longer than (we, us).

Part Two: Correct any pronoun errors that appear in the following sentences. If a sentence has no pronoun errors, label it *C* for *correct*. These sentences cover rules from Lessons 17 and 18.

7. Our boss decided to give both Tim and I a promotion.

8. This new assignment will be an interesting challenge for you and her.

9. Will you be inviting my roommate and myself to your graduation?

10. Between you and I, we'll get all the work done on time.

11. Us artists need to find a gallery to display our work.

12. The winners of the contest were Max and me.

13. Please let her and I go to the front of the line.

14. Let Mark pay the bill because you have less money than him.

15. The children and me are going to the county fair this weekend.

Harcourt, Inc.

16. The fair has a lot of interesting attractions for them and me.

17. Of course, I like the arts and crafts exhibits more than them.

18. This year, they're all old enough to go on the rides by themselfs.

19. My son he has been talking about the roller coaster all week.

20. He thinks his sisters are more nervous about the ride than him.

EXERCISE
18B

In the essay below, cross out the pronoun errors and replace them with the correct forms. This exercise covers Lessons 17 and 18.

Have you ever learned a skill by first watching someone and then doing what he did? I learned to ski this way many years ago. I went to June Mountain in the California Sierras with my brother Alan. He was always a better athlete than me, so sports were always more enjoyable for him. Doing anything that involved coordination was easier for him than for I. Alan, he is a real athlete. I am not.

At June Mountain, Alan enrolled both he and me in a local ski school that used what was called the "graduated length method." This meant that Alan and me started out on really short skis so we would not fall and hurt ourselfs while we were learning the basics. Alan was impatient with this method because he was convinced he needed less time than me to master skiing. I, however, was content to start as slowly as possible.

The first day was horrible. Alan was braver than me in trying out the downhill runs. Inevitably, I fell more than him. He laughed at me, and I felt myself growing resentful that he was so much more adept than me.

However, on the second day, something happened. Alan, he seemed to lose some of his edge while I began to feel better about me as a skier. Then, the instructor asked Alan and myself to ski a rather steep and twisting run. We started out together, but, to my surprise, I finished faster than him. Alan was upset because he had always assumed he was a better athlete than me. However, I was very pleased with myself and the progress I had made.

C H A P T E R 19

AGREEMENT OF PRONOUNS WITH THEIR ANTECEDENTS

AGREEMENT IN NUMBER

Like nouns, pronouns may be either singular or plural, depending on whether they refer to one or more than one person or thing. Following are the subject, object, and possessive pronouns you have learned, divided into singular and plural categories.

Singular Pronouns

Subject	*Object*	*Possessive*
I	me	my, mine
you	you	your, yours
he	him	his
she	her	her, hers
it	it	its

Plural Pronouns

Subject	*Object*	*Possessive*
we	us	our, ours
you	you	your, yours
they	them	their, theirs

Just as a subject must agree in number with its verb, a pronoun must agree in number with its antecedent. (The **antecedent,** you will remember, is the noun to which the pronoun refers.) In other words, if the antecedent is *singular,* the pronoun must be *singular.* If the antecedent is *plural,* the pronoun must be *plural.*

Study the following sentences, in which both the pronouns and their antecedents have been italicized.

Because the *teacher* is ill, *she* will not be at school today.

Because the *teachers* are ill, *they* will not be at school today.

Obviously, few people would make pronoun agreement errors in the above sentences because *teacher* is clearly singular, and *teachers* is clearly plural. However, people often make pronoun agreement errors in cases like the following:

INCORRECT   If an airline *passenger* wants to be certain not to miss their flight, *they* should arrive at the airport an hour before the scheduled departure time.

CORRECT   If an airline *passenger* wants to be certain not to miss the flight, *he* should arrive at the airport an hour before the scheduled departure time.

Because *passengers* include females as well as males, it would be equally correct to say:

If an airline *passenger* wants to be certain not to miss the flight, *she* should arrive at the airport an hour before the scheduled departure time.

If an airline *passenger* wants to be certain not to miss the flight, *she* or *he* should arrive at the airport an hour before the scheduled departure time.

For a more detailed discussion of the *his* or *her* construction, see the section on "Avoiding Sexist Language" on pages 174–175.

Notice the differences in these sentences:

INCORRECT   Each *student* brought *their* notebook.

CORRECT   Each *student* brought *his* notebook.

Harcourt, Inc.

What causes people to make mistakes like these? The mistakes may occur because when a writer describes a *passenger,* she is thinking of *passengers* (plural) in general. Similarly, a writer may think of a *student* as *students* in general. Nevertheless, because *passenger* and *student* are singular nouns, they must be used with singular pronouns.

Notice that if several pronouns refer to the same antecedent, *all* of the pronouns must agree in number with that antecedent.

Before Mike begins to run, *he* always stretches *his* muscles.

If the *students* don't review *their* lessons, *they* won't do well on their final exams.

Another common pronoun agreement error involves **indefinite pronouns.** As you learned in Lesson 6 on subject-verb agreement, indefinite pronouns are *singular* and require *singular* verbs. (For example, "Everyone *is* happy," *not* "Everyone *are* happy.") Similarly, when indefinite pronouns are used as antecedents, they require *singular* subject, object, and possessive pronouns.

The following words are singular indefinite pronouns:

anybody, anyone, anything

each, each one

either, neither

everybody, everyone, everything

nobody, no one, nothing

somebody, someone, something

Notice the use of singular pronouns with these words.

Everyone did as *he* pleased.

Somebody has forgotten *her* purse.

Either of the choices has *its* disadvantages.

In informal spoken English, plural pronouns are often used with indefinite pronoun antecedents. However, this construction is generally not considered appropriate in formal speech or writing.

INFORMAL   *Somebody* should let you borrow *their* book.

FORMAL   *Somebody* should let you borrow *his* book.

In some sentences, an indefinite pronoun is so clearly plural in meaning that a singular pronoun sounds awkward with it. For example,

Everyone on this block must be wealthy because *they* all drive a Lexus or a Mercedes-Benz.

A better wording for this sentence would be:

The people on this block must be wealthy because they all drive a Lexus or a Mercedes-Benz.

AVOIDING SEXIST LANGUAGE

Although matching singular pronouns with singular antecedents is a grammatical problem, a usage problem may occur if the antecedent of a singular pronoun refers to both genders. In the past, singular masculine pronouns were used to refer to antecedents such as *worker* or *student* even if these antecedents included women as well as men. Now, many writers prefer to use forms that include both sexes, such as *he or she* or *his or her* to avoid excluding women.

Each student must bring his or her books to class each day.

Everyone needs to consider his or her options.

A simpler format is to make both the pronoun and its antecedent plural.

All *students* must bring *their* books to class each day.

Avoiding sexist language is a problem of usage, not of grammar. To simplify the rules for you while you are still studying grammar, most of the exercises in this unit will offer you the choice between one singular pronoun (either masculine or feminine) and one plural pronoun. For example,

Each orchestra member needs (her, their) instrument.

Everyone should mark (his, their) ballot.

Which pronouns would be correct in the following sentences according to the rules of formal English usage?

Neither of the professors had (her, their) office hours at a time convenient for me.

Someone has forgotten to turn off (his, their) car's lights.

Each of the actors knew (her, their) part well.

An astronaut must spend hours training for (his, their) career.

Harcourt, Inc.

Each of the children said that (she, they) had loved the theatrical performance.

Only a member may bring (her, their) friends to the event.

AGREEMENT IN PERSON

In grammar, pronouns are classified into groups called **persons. First person** refers to the person who is speaking. **Second person** is the person being spoken to. **Third person** is the person or thing being spoken about. Below is a chart of subject pronouns grouped according to person.

	Singular	*Plural*
first person	I	we
second person	you	you
third person	he, she, it	they

All nouns are considered third person (either singular or plural) because nouns can be replaced by third-person pronouns (for example, *Susie = she; a car = it; babysitters = they*).

Just as a pronoun and its antecedent must agree in number, they must also agree in person. Agreement in person becomes a problem only when the second-person pronoun *you* is incorrectly used with a third-person antecedent. Study the following examples:

INCORRECT	If *anyone* wants to vote, *you* must register first.
CORRECT	If *anyone* wants to vote, *he or she* must register first.
INCORRECT	When *drivers* get caught in a traffic jam, *you* become impatient.
CORRECT	When *drivers* get caught in a traffic jam, *they* become impatient.

This type of mistake is called a **shift in person** and is considered a serious grammatical error.

In addition to avoiding shifts in person within individual sentences, you should try to be consistent in your use of person when you are writing essays. In general, an entire essay is written in the same person. If, for example, you are writing an essay about the special problems faced by students who work full-time, you will probably use either the first or the third person. You should avoid shifts into the second person (*you*) because *you* refers to the reader of your paper and not to the students you are writing about.

INCORRECT	*Students* who work full-time have special concerns. For example, *you* must arrange *your* classes to fit *your* work schedule.
CORRECT	*Students* who work full-time have special concerns. For example, *they* must arrange *their* classes to fit *their* work schedule.

Circle the pronoun that correctly completes each sentence.

The zoo has extended its hours so that patrons may visit when (your, his, their) schedules allow.

Participants must bring tickets to the front office, or else (you, he, they) will forfeit (your, his, their) chance to win the free gift.

Pay close attention; (your, his, their) final exam grade depends on following the directions carefully.

Harcourt, Inc.

EXERCISE
19A

If a sentence contains a pronoun error, cross out the incorrect pronoun and write in the correct form. Some sentences may contain more than one error. If a sentence contains no pronoun errors, label it *C* for *correct*. Apply the rules of formal English usage. Sentences 1–10 cover only the rules from Lesson 19.

1. Each of these new apartment buildings has their own swimming pool.

2. A driver must show proof of insurance before you register your car.

3. If a student misses the final exam, they will get a grade of "incomplete" at the end of the term.

4. Doesn't anybody have their cell phone here?

5. If a patient needs to see an obstetrician, they need a referral from their primary physician.

6. After the election, everyone was talking about the way they voted.

7. Either my husband or his brother will lend you their car.

8. Everybody who plans to attend the conference must pay their registration fee by tomorrow.

9. Each of the beauty pageant contestants has her own chaperone.

10. Doesn't anyone know how their state senator voted on the new tax bill?

The following sentences cover rules from Lessons 17–19.

11. Although I drive a larger car than he, I get much better mileage than him.

12. If it were up to we employees, everyone would have three weeks of paid vacation per year.

13. Jerry always gets better grades in French than me because he lived in Paris for a year as a child.

14. The office manager asked Susan and I to work overtime this week.

15. Does everyone realize they must register for classes by Wednesday?

16. Just tell him and me what to do next.

17. My mother is a much better cook than me.

18. Aren't you and him going to pay for this meal?

19. The salesman tried to get my mother and myself to invest in a uranium mine.

20. My mother thinks an elderly widow like herself should invest their money in something safer, like Treasury bonds.

Harcourt, Inc.

EXERCISE
19B

If a sentence contains an error in pronoun usage, cross out the incorrect pronoun and write in the correct form. Some sentences contain more than one error. If a sentence contains no pronoun errors, label it *C* for *correct*. Apply the rules of formal English usage. This exercise covers Lessons 17–19.

1. Each one of the players must bring their uniforms to practice.

2. I baked those pies for you and he.

3. She dances more gracefully than me.

4. Many of we voters were disturbed by the court's decisions.

5. Neither he nor me wants to work on a holiday.

6. My father and myself take a walk together after dinner.

7. Everybody should be sure to wash their hands often during flu season.

8. Somebody left their backpack in the hallway!

9. Either she or we will bring dessert for the dinner party.

10. Students must bring your books to each and every class meeting.

11. The innkeeper made hot chocolate for Bob and I.

12. According to Meg and he, this restaurant gets A1 ratings!

13. He likes snowboarding a lot more than me!

14. Christmas makes my friends and me very happy.

15. Gossip often leads to someone getting their feelings hurt.

16. My friends and me, however, have trouble not listening to stories about other friends.

17. Most serious athletes spend their free time on their sport.

18. If a person practices regularly, they will get accomplished at the task.

19. Everybody says they're happy, but how many people really are?

20. Between you and me, reading is my favorite sport!

Harcourt, Inc.

20

ORDER OF PRONOUNS AND SPELLING OF POSSESSIVES

Order of Pronouns

When you are referring to someone else and to yourself in the same sentence, mention the other person's name (or the pronoun that replaces the name) before you mention your own.

INCORRECT	*I* and *George* are brothers.
CORRECT	*George* and *I* are brothers.
INCORRECT	You can borrow five dollars from *me* or *her*.
CORRECT	You can borrow five dollars from *her* or *me*.

The construction is actually not a rule of grammar; rather, it is considered a matter of courtesy.

Possessive Pronouns

Here is a list of possessive pronouns that you have already studied. This time, look carefully at how they are spelled and punctuated.

	Singular	*Plural*
first person	my, mine	our, ours
second person	your, yours	your, yours
third person	his	their, theirs
	her, hers	
	its	

Possessive pronouns do not contain apostrophes.

INCORRECT	The beach blanket was *her's*.
CORRECT	The beach blanket was *hers*.

Be especially careful not to confuse the possessive pronoun *its* with the contraction *it's* (it is).

INCORRECT	The car wouldn't start because *it's* battery was dead.
CORRECT	The car wouldn't start because *its* battery was dead.

Another source of confusion is the apostrophe, which indicates the omitted letters in contractions. For example, the apostrophe in *don't* represents the missing *o* from *do not*. Some contractions of pronouns and verbs have the same pronunciations as certain possessive pronouns. These pairs of words sound alike but differ in meaning. Don't confuse them in your writing.

who's–whose

Who's he? = *Who is* he?
Whose magazine is this? (possessive)

you're–your

You're looking well. = *You are* looking well.
Your car has a flat tire. (possessive)

they're–their

They're coming to the party. = *They are* coming to the party.
Their exhibit won the prize. (possessive)

Harcourt, Inc.

Circle the pronoun that correctly completes each sentence.

That dog is (hers, her's).

(Whose, Who's) car is blocking the driveway?

The team just received (its, it's) award.

(Your, You're) a happy person.

The new house is (theirs, their's).

A final note: When you do pronoun exercises, or when you use pronouns in your own writing, remember to apply the rules you have learned. If you rely on what "sounds right," your instincts may only supply those pronouns that would be appropriate in *informal* English.

EXERCISE
20A

If a sentence contains a pronoun error, cross out the incorrect pronoun and write in the correct form. Some sentences may contain more than one error. If a sentence contains no pronoun errors, mark it *C* for *correct*. Apply the rules of formal English usage. Sentences 1–10 cover only the rules from Lesson 20.

1. We try to return each pet to it's rightful owner.

2. If you have any questions, ask I or my partner for assistance.

3. The actor who's latest role was just nominated for an Academy Award is now in great demand.

4. Is that purse Emily's or your's?

5. Their always late, but they never admit the fault is their's.

6. Your never going to save money unless you have a budget.

7. That dog has its teeth bared, and its probably ready to attack.

8. Can you tell me whose the doctor on call today?

9. This argument is between me and you.

10. That car isn't her's; its mine.

Sentences 11–20 cover rules from Lessons 17–20.

11. I have no idea who's car is blocking our driveway.

12. Our family's Thanksgiving dinner will be prepared by myself and my sister-in-law.

13. People prefer to work with Sally rather than Jim because she's more dependable than him.

14. If passengers are taking an international flight, you should arrive at the airport at least two hours early.

15. Is the college band taking the same bus as us football players?

16. If you were as uncoordinated as me, you wouldn't want to go skiing either.

17. It's unfair of our boss to ask Tom and I to work on holidays just because we are the only unmarried employees in the office.

18. We must make sure that each of the players on the women's basketball team has passed their pre-season medical exam.

19. Why don't they ever know what their doing?

20. Its up to you and me to decide whose the winner of the art contest.

Harcourt, Inc.

Exercise
20B

If a sentence contains an error in pronoun usage, cross out the incorrect pronoun and write in the correct form. Some sentences may contain more than one error. If a sentence contains no pronoun errors, label it *C* for *correct*. Apply the rules of formal English usage. This exercise covers Lessons 17–20.

1. Whose watching the children?

2. They want us to make they're vacation a good one.

3. If a citizen fails to vote, they give up their most important civic duty.

4. She is sure that antique watch is her's.

5. Who's coming to the party tomorrow night?

6. Each student turned in their exam before leaving the room.

7. No one knows more about cooking than her.

8. That puppy loves it's master.

9. He and John want to be computer programmers.

10. I admire the way they plan their futures.

11. Its wise to have an action plan about your education.

12. For me and Bill, our plans are to marry soon.

13. Who's plans are those?

UNIT REVIEW

PRONOUN USAGE

Part One. Correct any errors in pronoun usage that you find in the following sentences. Cross out the incorrect pronouns, and write in the correct forms. Some sentences may have more than one error. If a sentence has no pronoun errors, mark it *C* for *correct*. Apply the rules of formal English usage. This exercise covers the rules in Lessons 17–20.

1. Our company's new ten-hour work day is causing problems for some of my co-workers and I.

2. Some of we mothers need to get home early enough to fix dinner for our families.

3. In my family, it is me who does most of the cooking, not my husband.

4. My children are eight and ten years old, and I can't rely on them to prepare a whole meal for themselfs.

5. Many of my co-workers and myself would prefer returning to an eight-hour day.

6. Our boss says the company needs to operate more efficiently and that everyone has to make sacrifices to keep their job.

7. Personally, I think its a lot easier for my boss to talk about sacrifices than it is for my co-workers and I.

8. Its true that the new ten-hour day schedule gives we employees an extra day off.

9. But after working four ten-hour days, we are too tired to enjoy ourselfs.

10. I and two of my friends are thinking about circulating a petition to ask for a return to the eight-hour day.

11. We're not sure, though, whose willing to sign a petition.

12. Everyone who's signature is on the petition could get in trouble with the boss.

13. Everyone must think about the potential danger before they decide to sign.

14. Its especially hard to risk your job when your the sole support of your family.

15. I think we should have a meeting of just us workers to decide what to do next.

16. Our boss has been here for only two years, so most of the employees have worked for the company a lot longer than him.

17. Just between you and I, some of us don't think he has very good judgment.

18. But he would argue that he's just doing his job and that we should do our's.

19. In his opinion, anyone who doesn't like the new work schedule should find themselves a new job.

Part Two. Construct your own sentences using pronouns according to the following directions.

20. Write a sentence containing a comparison with the conjunction *than* and a *subject pronoun.*

_____

21. Write a sentence that has two subjects: a noun and a *subject pronoun.*

_____

22. Write a sentence about yourself, using the pronoun *myself* correctly.

_____

23. Write a sentence containing *everyone* as a subject and a *possessive pronoun* agreeing with *everyone.*

_____

24. Write a sentence using both *your* and *you're.*

_____

25. Write a sentence using *who's.*

_____

26. Write a sentence using both *its* and *it's.*

_____

27. Write a sentence using *whose.*

_____

28. Write a sentence using the pronoun *us* followed by a plural noun.

_____

29. Write a sentence using the pronoun *we* followed by a plural noun.

_____

UNIT 6

CAPITALIZATION, MORE PUNCTUATION, PLACEMENT OF MODIFIERS, PARALLEL STRUCTURE, AND IRREGULAR VERBS

21

CAPITALIZATION

The general principle behind capitalization is that **proper nouns** (names of *specific* persons, places, or things) are capitalized. **Common nouns** (names of *general* persons, places, or things) are *not* capitalized.

Study the following sentences, each of which illustrates a rule of capitalization.

1. Capitalize all parts of a person's name.

That man is *John Allen Ford.*

2. Capitalize the titles of relatives only when the titles precede the person's name or when they take the place of a person's name.

Our favorite relative is *Uncle Max.*

Are you ready, *Mother?*

Harcourt, Inc.

but

My *mother* and *father* are retired.

The same rule applies to professional titles.

We saw *Doctor Johnson* at the market.

but

I must see a *doctor* soon.

3. Capitalize the names of streets, cities, and states.

Deirdre moved to 418 *Palm Avenue, Placerville, California.*

4. Capitalize the names of countries, languages, and ethnic groups.

The two languages spoken most frequently in *Switzerland* are *German* and *French*, but some *Swiss* also speak *Italian.*

5. Capitalize the names of specific buildings, geographical features, schools, and other institutions.

They visited the *Tower of London*, the *Thames River*, and *Cambridge University.*

6. Capitalize the days of the week, the months of the year, and the names of holidays. Do *not* capitalize the names of the seasons of the year.

Monday, February 14, is *Valentine's Day.*
My favorite time of the year is the *fall*, especially *November.*

7. Capitalize directions of the compass only when they refer to specific regions.

Her accent revealed that she had been brought up in the *South.*
Philadelphia is *south* of New York City.

8. Capitalize the names of companies and brand names but not the names of the products themselves.

General Foods Corporation manufactures *Yuban* coffee.
We love *Campbell's* soups.

9. Capitalize the first word of every sentence.

10. Capitalize the subject pronoun *I*.

11. Capitalize the first word of a title and all other words in the title except for articles (*a, an, the*) and except for conjunctions and prepositions that have fewer than five letters.

   I loved the novel *The House of the Seven Gables* by Nathaniel Hawthorne.

   I enjoy reading the short essay "Once More to the Lake."

12. Capitalize the names of academic subjects only if they are already proper nouns or if they are common nouns followed by a course number.

   Her schedule of classes includes *c*alculus, *E*nglish, and *P*sychology 101.

13. Capitalize the names of specific historical events, such as wars, revolutions, religious and political movements, and specific eras.

   The *R*oaring *T*wenties came to an end with the start of the *D*epression.

   Martin Luther was a key figure in the *P*rotestant *R*eformation.

   For most of us the last great war was not *W*orld *W*ar II, but the *V*ietnam *W*ar.

Harcourt, Inc.

EXERCISE
21A

Add capital letters to the following sentences wherever they are necessary.

1. The first wife of an american president to be elected to the senate of the united states was hillary rodham clinton.

2. this summer my mother and father will be visiting my aunt sarah in portland, oregon, and touring the rest of the pacific northwest.

3. In belgium, some of the population speaks flemish, and others speak french.

4. While you're in boston, be sure to visit the old north church, which was mentioned in the poem "paul revere's ride" by henry wadsworth longfellow.

5. another item of historical interest is the ship known as *old ironsides,* which dates back to america's war of 1812 with the british.

6. One of the nation's most well-known corporations is proctor & gamble, which manufactures a wide variety of products ranging from tide detergent to folger's coffee to cover girl cosmetics.

7. the film *crouching tiger, hidden dragon* showed actors performing a variety of chinese martial arts.

8. Two of the busiest times for air travel are the thanksgiving and christmas holidays.

9. Our family spends a lot of money on phone bills because half of us live in california and the rest of our relatives live in new england.

10. Many people think of san francisco as being directly north of los angeles, but it is also much farther west.

11. my grandparents are very thrifty because they grew up during the hard economic times of the depression.

12. One of the most famous novels that came out of this period was john steinbeck's *the grapes of wrath*.

13. A famous folk singer of that era was Woody guthrie, who wrote the songs "this land is your land" and "so long, it's been good to know you."

14. Because my doctor was on vacation, i had to see a new physician, doctor robert bentley at daniel freeman hospital.

15. My history 11 instructor is lecturing this week on the changes in the american economy after world war II, and, by coincidence, so is my economics professor.

16. Many peruvian restaurants feature dishes influenced by spanish, inca, and chinese cuisine.

EXERCISE
21B

Add capital letters to the sentences in the following essay wherever they are necessary.

Shopping in the united states and shopping in europe represent two very different experiences. Last summer I traveled to france—to paris, to be exact—for the first time in twenty years. I was at first struck by how many changes had taken place in retail buying and selling habits. There were many more chain stores and discount outlets similar to american Wal-Marts and costcos, but the heart of french shopping was still the small shop owned and run by a single proprietor. This person sits majestically at the cash register or stands vigilantly behind the counter, watching each customer's every move. I am a professor of mathematics, a respectable american citizen, but parisian shopkeepers still treat me as if I were a potential shoplifter.

If one enters a french shop, as I entered the shop called la plume, one is expected to know exactly what one wants to buy. There is zero tolerance for entering the store and just browsing. The typical american response to the question, "Can I help you?" is the noncommittal "Just looking." This will not do in paris. There one must have an answer, and a specific one, to that question. "A fountain pen—an aurora or a mont blanc, I think," will do for an answer. After that answer, the proprietor will bring out those particular pens and lay them on the countertop for examination—one at a time, as if putting more than one before the customer might tempt him to slide a pen into his pocket before it is purchased.

Shopping in american stores is quite a different matter. I live in los angeles, california, and shop at many malls there. For example, in the northwest sector of the city, one can go to the beverly center, a large mall in which there are restaurants, movie theaters, and a great many shops. The beverly center is located on LaCienega boulevard and beverly boulevard. Across the street from it is yet another mall called the beverly connection, which also houses stores, restaurants, and movie theaters. I dislike both malls because the parking is a virtual nightmare. My favorite mall is actually in santa monica, california. It is called the third street promenade. Unlike the other two malls, this place is outdoors. It is a lot of fun because it is filled with street performers of all kinds. I love to sit at the restaurant la matisse, sip some coffee, and watch the world go by. In some ways, these moments remind me a little of paris—their human quality and more leisurely pace. Shopping, however, is always american.

Harcourt, Inc.

CHAPTER 22

More Punctuation

I n Lesson 10 you learned to put a comma after an introductory dependent clause. At certain other times, it is customary to separate other *introductory* material from an independent clause that follows it.

With joy in her heart, the actress gave her acceptance speech. (introductory prepositional phrase)

Watching the ocean, the swimmers were excited about the race. (introductory participial phrase)

Frightened by the noise, the children ran to their parents. (introductory participial phrase)

It is also customary to separate coordinate adjectives modifying the same noun. (Adjectives are *coordinate* if you can substitute *and* for the comma.)

Harcourt, Inc.

They own a *small, cozy* cottage.

or

They own a small and cozy cottage.

You learned in earlier lessons to use commas to set off appositives and parenthetical expressions. However, when the writer wishes to emphasize the importance or abruptness of such words, a **dash** may be used instead.

February—or maybe March—will be our last practice examination.

At the party, he sang our favorite songs—Broadway show tunes.

The **colon** is sometimes confused with the semicolon because of the similarity in names, but the two marks function differently. In addition to the colon's mechanical use to separate hours from minutes (8:45) and biblical chapters from verses (Genesis 2:5), this mark is frequently used to introduce lists, summaries, series, and quotations that may be of almost any length or form. (Notice that what follows the colon is not necessarily an independent clause; that is, it may be a fragment.)

He is studying three of the major modern American novelists: Hemingway, Fitzgerald, and Stein.

Two things are certain in life: death and taxes.

Shakespeare said it so well: "To thine own self be true."

An **apostrophe** with an *-s* (*'s* or *s'*) in nouns and indefinite pronouns makes those words possessive. For singular nouns or indefinite pronouns, add the apostrophe followed by *-s*.

Ben's games

the dog's dish

everyone's responsibility

a day's effort

Debbie and Allen's house

or

Debbie's and Allen's house

For most plural nouns (those ending in an *-s, -sh,* or *-z* sound), use the apostrophe alone.

Harcourt, Inc.

five cents' worth

the Phillips' house

the ladies' room

But for a plural noun not ending in an *-s, -sh,* or *-z* sound, add *'s.*

men*'s* issues

children*'s* toys

Sometimes possession is indicated by both the apostrophe and *of* in a prepositional phrase.

That CD *of* John*'s* is my favorite.

And a possessive may follow the word it modifies.

Is this CD John*'s*?

Direct quotations make writing vivid. Long direct quotations, as in research papers, are indented and single spaced, but most direct quotes are simply enclosed in **quotation marks.**

"Give me liberty, or give me death."

If the quotation is part of a longer sentence, it is set off by commas.

Patrick Henry said, "Give me liberty, or give me death."

"Friends," the speaker said, "it's time for a new beginning."

Three rules govern the use of quotation marks with other forms of punctuation:

1. The comma and period are always placed *inside* the quotation marks.

   "We love theater," he said, "but we can't afford it."

2. The colon and semicolon are always placed *outside* the quotation marks.

   I love the song "Blue"; it was recorded by LeAnn Rimes.

3. Question marks, exclamation marks, and dashes are placed *inside* the quotation marks if they apply only to the quoted material and *after* the quotation marks if they apply to the whole sentence.

"Is dinner almost ready?" asked Beth.

Did Shakespeare say, "The ripeness is all"?

You may have noticed in the discussion of capitalization that some titles are punctuated with quotation marks ("Once More to the Lake"), and some titles are shown in italics (*The House of the Seven Gables*). The choice between these two ways to indicate titles is generally based on the length of the work. The titles of short works, such as songs, short poems and stories, essays and articles in periodicals, and episodes of a series are put between *quotation marks*. The titles of longer works, such as full-length books and the names of newspapers, magazines, movies, and television shows, and the titles of complete volumes or complete series are put in *italics*.

Italics are a special slanted typeface used by printers. In a handwritten or type-written paper, italics must be indicated by **underlining.**

We read the chapter "No Name Woman" from Maxine Hong Kingston's *The Woman Warrior.*

I love the song "Summertime" from *Porgy and Bess.*

Did you see the episode "The Coming of Shadows" on the television series *Babylon 5?*

The *Los Angeles Times* printed an article titled "Upsetting Our Sense of Self" on the way cloning may influence how we think about our identity.

EXERCISE
22A

Add commas, colons, dashes, quotation marks, apostrophes, and italics to the following sentences wherever they are needed. Indicate italics by *underlining*.

1. When purchasing homes in California buyers can consult seismic maps to see how prone various neighborhoods might be to severe earthquake damage.

2. There is one thing you should know about the town where you plan to live it sits directly on top of one of the state's most active earthquake faults.

3. I need to buy at least 1 million dollars worth of liability insurance.

4. This project is not just my responsibility but everyones.

5. Your fiancé Robert if that's what he calls himself is still dating my best friend.

6. I want to buy a small inexpensive car.

7. My favorite barbecue restaurant offers a choice of three side dishes baked beans, coleslaw, or potato salad.

8. Benjamin Franklin said There never was a good war or a bad peace.

9. The ballot is stronger than the bullet said Abraham Lincoln.

10. Brevity said Shakespeare is the soul of wit.

11. Newsweek published an article titled Oprah on Oprah, which featured a lengthy interview with celebrity Oprah Winfrey.

12. In the interview, Winfrey said I am a person who is aware of what my purpose is and what my gifts are.

13. Oprah's Book Club has featured the novels Paradise by Toni Morrison and The Poisonwood Bible by Barbara Kingsolver.

14. The orchestra played songs from old Broadway musicals, such as Tonight from the musical West Side Story.

15. West Side Story is a modern version of Shakespeare's Romeo and Juliet.

16. Tony and Marias fate in the musical is almost as tragic as Romeo and Juliets.

17. Hoping to strike it rich my neighbor bought a dozen state lottery tickets.

18. His chances of winning only one in two million are less than his chances of being struck by lightning.

19. In preparation for their midterm exam the class was assigned to read the short story A Worn Path from The Collected Stories of Eudora Welty.

20. How long will the exam be asked one of the students?

21. Did Alice Walker write the short story Everyday Use?

EXERCISE
22B

Add capital letters, commas, dashes, apostrophes, colons, quotation marks, and italics to the following sentences wherever they are necessary. Indicate italics by *underlining*.

even in the age of the personal computer perhaps even more so the large daily newspaper is an amazingly rich resource. In the new york times sunday edition, one enters a world of information, opinion, and images. "all the news that's fit to print" is the times's slogan; it is filled with mens and womens and childrens issues, with politicians quotes and actors observations. As Shakespeare asked Whats in a name? Well, the times name is certainly appropriate; it captures the fact that the papers intention is to represent the times in which we live. There is one thing the new york times doesn't have comic strips!

As one might suspect not all national newspaper offerings are as informative. There are many odd publications, like the national enquirer, that offer items that might or might not be "news." This we do know their articles are interesting. Certainly, items with titles like Killer hedgehogs invade farmers' market spark an immediate interest in the readers mind. Though funny and interesting, these articles are not taken seriously as real news. In contrast, when people want to vouch for the truth of a news item, they often say I read it in the new york times!

There are also daily newspapers whose owners are sometimes local residents. these newspapers report what might be considered high-level gossip, such as marriages and engagements and who's going out with whom. In these papers it is the local police report stories that are most interesting, such as Man apprehended with missing store's mannequin or Dog's bed disappears. Such odd stories tell of small-town lives, of the ongoing human drama that would never make national headlines. You never know what to expect in our paper stated one individual.

We need all three kinds of newspapers because societys interests are diverse, and diverse ways of expressing those interests are needed. The new york times, national enquirer, and village news are all necessary to the nations love of and need for information.

Harcourt, Inc.

CHAPTER 23

MISPLACED AND DANGLING MODIFIERS

Modifiers are words that are used to describe other words in a sentence. A modifier may be a single word, a phrase, or a clause. (Adjective clauses are discussed in Lesson 15.) Examples of some of the more common types of modifiers are given below. Circle the word that each italicized modifier describes.

ADJECTIVE	He drank a cup of *black* coffee.
ADJECTIVE CLAUSE	The woman *who is dressed in blue* is the bride's mother.
PREPOSITIONAL PHRASE	*With the help of a nurse,* the patient was able to take a shower.

The words you should have circled are *coffee,* which is modified by "black," *woman,* which is modified by "who is dressed in blue," and *patient,* which is modified by "with the help of a nurse."

Another type of modifier is a **participial phrase.** A participial phrase begins with a participle. A **participle** is a verb form that functions as an adjective. There are two kinds of participles. **Present participles** are formed by adding *-ing* to the main verb (for example, *walking, knowing, seeing.*) **Past participles** are the verb forms that are used with the helping verb *have* (have *walked,* have *known,* have *seen*). Circle the word that each of the following participial phrases modifies.

Looking excited, the child begged for more presents.

The woman *dressed very expensively* is a famous model.

The words that you should have circled are *child* and *woman.*

If you look back at all the words that you have circled so far in this lesson, you will notice that although modifiers sometimes precede and sometimes follow the words they describe, they are in all cases placed as closely as possible to the word that they describe. Failure to place a modifier in the correct position in a sentence results in an error known as a **misplaced modifier.**

MISPLACED	He told a joke to his friends *that no one liked.* (Did no one like his friends?)
CORRECT	He told a joke *that no one liked* to his friends.
MISPLACED	Sue always uses pencils for her math exams *with extremely fine points.* (Do the exams have extremely fine points?)
CORRECT	Sue always uses pencils *with extremely fine points* for her math exams.

Correct the misplaced modifiers in the following sentences.

The citizen informed the sheriff that the thief had escaped by phone.

The child clutched the old teddy bear with tears rolling down his face.

A firm called Threshold provides companions for people who are dying at $7.50 per hour.

An error related to the misplaced modifier is the **dangling modifier.** A dangling modifier sometimes occurs when a participial phrase is placed at the beginning of a sentence. A participial phrase in this position *must describe the subject of the following clause.* If the subject of the clause cannot logically perform the action described in the participial phrase, the phrase is said to "dangle" (to hang loosely, without a logical connection).

Harcourt, Inc.

DANGLING	*While typing a letter,* my contact lens popped out. (This sentence suggests that the *contact lens* was typing the letter.)
CORRECT	*While I was typing a letter,* my contact lens popped out.
DANGLING	*Trying to save money,* Susan's clothes were bought at a thrift shop. (This sentence suggests that Susan's *clothes* were trying to save money.)
CORRECT	Trying to save money, *Susan* bought her clothes at a thrift shop.

Notice that there are several ways to correct dangling modifiers. You may add a noun or pronoun to the sentence to provide a word that the modifier can logically describe, or you may reword the entire sentence. *However, simply reversing the order of the dangling modifier and the rest of the sentence does not correct the error.*

DANGLING	*While sleeping,* her phone rang.
STILL DANGLING	Her phone rang while sleeping.
CORRECT	While she was sleeping, her phone rang.

Revise the following sentences so that they no longer contain dangling modifiers.

After standing all day, my feet look forward to sitting down.

While vacuuming the carpet, the fuse blew.

While taking the final exam, my pen ran out of ink.

By eating well, your life will be prolonged.

Because misplaced and dangling modifiers create confusing and even absurd sentences, you should be careful to avoid them in your writing.

Harcourt, Inc.

EXERCISE
23A

Part One: Rewrite the following sentences so that they do not contain misplaced or dangling modifiers. Some sentences may have more than one error. If a sentence has no modifier errors, mark it *C* for *correct*.

1. By the age of ten, Bob's parents were divorced.

   _____

   _____

2. The television commercial showed a beautiful young woman driving an expensive sports car with a Rolex watch.

   _____

   _____

3. Some of my best ideas occur to me while driving to work.

   _____

   _____

4. Date trees were planted by farmers in the desert resistant to drought.

   _____

   _____

5. Kate's toothache went away while waiting in the dentist's office.

   _____

   _____

6. The fast-food restaurant was sued for serving coffee to a customer that was hot enough to cause serious burns.

   _____

   _____

7. Hoping to win the tournament, the coach held extra practice sessions for his team.

   _____

   _____

8. I put the leftover food down the garbage disposal that was spoiled.

_____

_____

9. After playing with his children, Rob's back muscles were sore.

_____

_____

10. Her migraine headaches sometimes begin after arguing with her husband.

_____

_____

Part Two: Construct five sentences of your own, using the modifiers listed below in the positions indicated in the sentences. Make certain that your modifiers are not misplaced and are not dangling.

11. _____while studying for an exam.

12. Trying to impress his new girlfriend, _____.

13. After winning the state lottery, _____.

14. _____ by investing their money wisely.

15. _____ that had been stolen.

Harcourt, Inc.

EXERCISE
23B

Some of the following sentences contain misplaced modifiers or dangling modifiers. Rewrite these sentences. If a sentence is correctly constructed, label it *C* for *correct*.

1. Jim sang rock songs in the club from the 1970s.

_____

_____

2. Before going home, the bill was paid.

_____

_____

3. She baked John a pie with some reservations.

_____

_____

4. Performing flawlessly, the actors delivered a magnificent performance.

_____

_____

5. Laughing wildly, his eyes bugged out!

_____

_____

6. The horse leapt over the fence with a swift motion.

_____

_____

7. After studying hard, her finals seemed easy.

_____

_____

8. We brought roses to the party which we had purchased earlier.

_____

_____

9. He built a cottage for his true love out of the stones in the garden.

_____

_____

10. When blasting the radio, the walls vibrated.

_____

_____

11. With respect for one another, the candidates shook hands and smiled.

_____

_____

Harcourt, Inc.

C H A P T E R 24

PARALLEL STRUCTURE

The term **parallel structure** means that similar ideas should be expressed in similar grammatical structures. For example, Benjamin Franklin quoted the following proverb:

Early to bed and early to rise make a man healthy, wealthy, and wise.

This proverb is a good illustration of parallel structure. It begins with two similar phrases, "Early to bed" and "early to rise," and it ends with a series of three similar words (they are all adjectives): *healthy, wealthy,* and *wise.*

In contrast, the following two versions of the same proverb contain some words that are *not* parallel.

Early to bed and early *rising* make a man healthy, wealthy, and wise.

Early to bed and early to rise make a man healthy, wealthy, and *give him wisdom.*

Harcourt, Inc.

Therefore, these last two sentences are *not* properly constructed.

Because there are many different grammatical structures in the English language, the possibilities for constructing nonparallel sentences may appear to be almost unlimited. Fortunately, you do not have to be able to identify all the grammatical structures in a sentence to tell whether or not that sentence has parallel structure. Sentences that lack parallel structure are usually so awkward that they are easy to recognize.

NOT PARALLEL	My chores are *washing dishes, cleaning the bathrooms, and to water the lawn.*
PARALLEL	My chores are *washing dishes, cleaning the bathrooms, and watering the lawn.*
NOT PARALLEL	I expect you *to read* all the assignments, *to complete* all the exercises, and *that you should attend every class.*
PARALLEL	I expect you *to read* all the assignments, *to complete* all the exercises, and *to attend* every class.
NOT PARALLEL	The fortune teller said my husband would be *tall, dark,* and *have good looks.*
PARALLEL	The fortune teller said my husband would be *tall, dark,* and *good looking.*

Revise each of the following sentences so that it is parallel in structure.

The steak was tough, overcooked, and had no taste.

The school emphasizes the basic skills of reading, how to write, and arithmetic.

He spent his day off playing tennis and went to the beach.

Your blind date is attractive and has intelligence.

Some errors in parallel structure occur when a writer is not careful in the use of correlative conjunctions. **Correlative conjunctions** are conjunctions that occur in pairs, such as:

both . . . and

either . . . or

neither . . . nor

not only . . . but also

Because these conjunctions occur in pairs, they are usually used to compare two ideas. For example,

Harcourt, Inc.

My professor suggests that I *not only* study more *but also* attend class more regularly.

Correctly used, correlative conjunctions will structure a sentence in effective parallel form.

The rule for using correlative conjunctions is that the conjunctions *must be placed as closely as possible to the words that are being compared.* For example,

I must go home *either* today *or* tomorrow.

not

I *either* must go home today *or* tomorrow.

Study the following examples of correctly and incorrectly placed correlative conjunctions.

INCORRECT	He *not only* got an "A" in math *but also* in English.
CORRECT	He got an "A" *not only* in math *but also* in English.
INCORRECT	She *neither* is a good housekeeper *nor* a good cook.
CORRECT	She is *neither* a good housekeeper *nor* a good cook.

Correct the misplaced correlative conjunctions in the following sentences.

He both collects stamps and coins.

She neither eats meat nor dairy products.

He both plays the piano and the flute.

My daughter not only has had chicken pox but also mumps.

Harcourt, Inc.

EXERCISE
24A

Rewrite any sentences that lack parallel structure. If a sentence is already parallel, label it C for *correct*.

1. That restaurant has poorly prepared food, high prices, and its service is slow.

   _____

   _____

2. The doctor told her patient to eat less, exercise more, and that he should stop smoking.

   _____

   _____

3. If you win the contest, you either get a Hawaiian vacation or $5,000 in cash.

   _____

   _____

4. The college offered Fred an athletic scholarship because he excelled both in football and baseball.

   _____

   _____

5. On the application form, please list your name, where you live, and your phone number.

   _____

   _____

6. Today's beauty pageant contestants not only must have beauty but also be poised and have intelligence.

   _____

   _____

7. Tell the detective where you were last night, whom you were with, and how long you were there.

   _____

   _____

Harcourt, Inc.

8. Why would you want to see a film with poor acting, unrealistic special effects, and a plot that is boring?

_____

_____

9. His goals are graduating from college and to get a good job.

_____

_____

10. An old saying warns us about hearing no evil, seeing no evil, and to speak no evil.

_____

_____

Harcourt, Inc.

Exercise
24B

Rewrite any sentences that lack parallel structure or that contain misplaced or dangling modifiers. If a sentence needs no revision, label it *C* for *correct*.

1. I love going to the mall, drinking hot tea, and to shop till I drop!

   _____

   _____

2. He walks either to school or rides his bike.

   _____

   _____

3. She was told to practice the piano each day and that she should listen to classical music.

   _____

   _____

4. They not only train in Europe but also in Japan.

   _____

   _____

5. Ben plays video games a lot, studies strategies a great deal, and listens to his MP3 player!

   _____

   _____

6. His agenda was to study hard at school, to get a very good job, and buying an expensive sports car.

   _____

   _____

7. They both run a small gift store and book publishing business.

   _____

   _____

8. After running the marathon, her legs gave out.

   _____

   _____

9. They hired a person who had initiative, drive, and who was enthusiastic.

_____

_____

10. The family not only rescued the puppies but also that litter of kittens.

_____

_____

11. They studied every night for their final examination with great dedication.

_____

_____

Harcourt, Inc.

IRREGULAR VERBS

Verbs have three **principal** (meaning "most important") **parts:** the *present* (which, when preceded by *to*, becomes the *infinitive*), the *past*, and the *past participle*.

The **present** form may stand alone as a main verb without any helping verb. For example,

I *like* movies.

We *watch* television each night.

It may also be preceded by a helping verb, such as *can, could, do, does, did, may, might, must, shall, should, will,* or *would*. (A list of helping verbs appears in Lesson 4.)

I *must talk* with you tomorrow.

Julia *should study* her vocabulary words.

However, the present form is not used after any forms of the helping verbs *have* (*has, have, had*) or *be* (*am, is, are, was, were, been*). The **past participle** (see below) is used after these verbs.

The **past** form is used alone as a main verb. It is *not* preceded by a helping verb when expressing the simple past tense.

They *ran* back to the classroom.

We *spelled* all the words correctly.

The **past participle** is preceded by at least one, and sometimes more than one, helping verb. The helping verb is often a form of *have* or *be*.

She *has spoken* very kindly of you.

The batter *was hit* by a ball.

Most English verbs are **regular.** A regular verb forms both its past and past participle by adding *-ed* to the present. (If the present already ends in *-e,* only a *-d* is added.)

Present	*Past*	*Past Participle*
walk	walked	walked
live	lived	lived

Any verb that does *not* form both its past and past participle by adding *-ed* or *-d* is considered **irregular.** For example,

Present	*Past*	*Past Participle*
fall	fell	fallen
give	gave	given
hide	hid	hidden

Because irregular verbs by definition have irregular spellings, you must *memorize* the spelling of their past and past participle forms. Irregular verbs include many of the most commonly used verbs in the English language (for example, *come, go, eat, drink, sit, stand*), so it is important to study them carefully.

Here is a list of some of the most commonly used irregular verbs. In addition to learning the verbs on this list, if you are not sure whether or not a verb is irregular, look it up in the dictionary. A good dictionary will list the principal parts of an irregular verb in addition to defining its meaning.

Harcourt, Inc.

Present	Past	Past Participle
beat	beat	beaten
begin	began	begun
bend	bent	bent
bleed	bled	bled
blow	blew	blown
break	broke	broken
bring	brought	brought
build	built	built
buy	bought	bought
catch	caught	caught
choose	chose	chosen
come	came	come
cut	cut	cut
do	did	done
draw	drew	drawn
drink	drank	drunk
drive	drove	driven
eat	ate	eaten
fall	fell	fallen
feed	fed	fed
feel	felt	felt
find	found	found
fly	flew	flown
freeze	froze	frozen
get	got	got *or* gotten
give	gave	given
go	went	gone
grow	grew	grown
have	had	had
hear	heard	heard
hide	hid	hidden
hit	hit	hit
hurt	hurt	hurt

Present	*Past*	*Past Participle*
keep	kept	kept
know	knew	known
lay	laid	laid
leave	left	left
lend	lent	lent
lie	lay	lain
lose	lost	lost
make	made	made
mean	meant	meant
meet	met	met
pay	paid	paid
put	put	put
read	read	read
ride	rode	ridden
ring	rang	rung
rise	rose	risen
run	ran	run
see	saw	seen
sell	sold	sold
send	sent	sent
set	set	set
shake	shook	shaken
shoot	shot	shot
sing	sang	sung
sink	sank	sunk
sit	sat	sat
sleep	slept	slept
speak	spoke	spoken
spend	spent	spent
spin	spun	spun
stand	stood	stood
steal	stole	stolen
stick	stuck	stuck

Harcourt, Inc.

Present	Past	Past Participle
swear	swore	sworn
swim	swam	swum
take	took	taken
teach	taught	taught
tear	tore	torn
tell	told	told
think	thought	thought
throw	threw	thrown
wear	wore	worn
weep	wept	wept
win	won	won
write	wrote	written

Notice that compound verbs follow the same pattern as their root form. For example,

be*come*	be*came*	be*come*
for*give*	for*gave*	for*given*
under*stand*	under*stood*	under*stood*

EXERCISE
25A

Fill each blank with the correct form (past or past participle) of the verb in parentheses. Try to do this exercise without looking at the list of verbs in your book.

1. (begin) I have not yet _____ my term paper.

2. (build) Their new home was _____ in less than six months.

3. (drive) My neighbor _____ me to work yesterday.

4. (hide) We have _____ all the children's Christmas presents.

5. (spend) He _____ all of his savings on a new computer.

6. (wear) Have you _____ that tuxedo more than once?

7. (steal) The car was _____ more than a month ago.

8. (meet) The committee _____ for two hours yesterday.

9. (read) I have _____ three novels for my literature class.

10. (send) He _____ you a package a week ago.

11. (fall) I am learning to ski, and I have _____ many times.

12. (hurt) Her feelings were _____ by what you said.

13. (keep) Has she _____ her maiden name after marriage?

14. (catch) He _____ a bad cold last week.

15. (find) The police have not _____ the robber yet.

16. (feel) The children _____ dizzy after they got off the roller coaster.

17. (swear) The witness _____ to tell the truth.

18. (write) This novel was _____ twenty years ago.

19. (swim) Jim _____ in the Olympic trials last year.

20. (sink) The *Titanic* _____ to the bottom of the ocean.

21. (sleep) The baby finally _____ the whole night through.

22. (take) My husband has _____ many photos of our family.

23. (ride) I have never _____ a motorcycle.

24. (pay) She _____ that bill last month.

25. (feed) The children should be _____ at five o'clock.

26. (choose) Have you _____ a major yet?

27. (grow) Last year I _____ corn in my backyard.

28. (rise) The audience _____ to its feet to sing the national anthem.

29. (lay) Those eggs were _____ only this morning.

30. (set) He _____ the groceries on the kitchen counter.

Harcourt, Inc.

EXERCISE
25B

Correct any verb form errors in the following sentences. Check the list of irregular verbs if you are unsure of the answer. If all the verb forms in the sentence are correct, place a *C* for *correct* in the left margin.

1. I have knowed that person for a long time.

2. If you are sleepy, just lie down and rest.

3. Did you putted the dishes back on the shelves?

4. They have ran that race each year.

5. The lady of the house had lain quietly in the dark before greeting her guests.

6. We thinked that the best way to lay carpet was to call in an expert!

7. I speaked with him often over the last several months.

8. Just lay down and take a load off your feet!

9. Have you broke your leg?

10. We all agreed that she teached very well.

11. Did you threw the ball over the fence?

12. The earthquake shaked our house a lot!

13. No one understanded what the professor was saying about Plato.

14. While studying irregular verbs, the students winned prizes for good study habits.

15. Their new car was stole last week.

Unit Review

Capitalization, More Punctuation, Placement of Modifiers, Parallel Structure, and Irregular Verbs

Part One. Add capital letters to the following passage wherever they are needed.

a few years ago, my niece and I spent our thanksgiving vacation in san francisco. we arrived on friday, november 27, on a united airlines flight from chicago. our aunt gail, who lives north of san francisco in the napa valley, met us at the airport.

with the help of a book titled *arthur frommer's guide to san francisco,* we visited many of the city's tourist attractions. on our first day in the city, we rode the powell street cable car to fisherman's wharf, where we had lunch at an italian restaurant named scoma's. then we walked a few blocks west to ghirardelli square. this area used to house a chocolate factory, but the buildings have been converted into shops and restaurants. however, you can still buy a ghirardelli chocolate bar. to end our day, we took a cruise around san francisco bay. the most exciting part of the cruise was passing under the golden gate bridge.

the next day we went to union square, where many of the city's finest stores are located. we were especially interested in gumps, which sells asian art and artifacts.

from union square it was only a short walk to chinatown, where we had dim sum (chinese dumplings) for lunch. we spent the rest of the afternoon on grant avenue, buying postcards and souvenirs for our relatives back home in the midwest.

that evening, our aunt and uncle took us to henri's room at the top, a restaurant on the forty-sixth floor of the hilton hotel. as we ate dinner, we had a panoramic view of the city, and we understood why san francisco is considered to be one of the most beautiful cities in the united states.

Part Two. Some of the following sentences contain misplaced or dangling modifiers; others lack parallel structure. Rewrite the incorrect sentences. If a sentence contains no structural errors, label it *C* for *correct*.

1. By using a microwave, my dinner is ready to eat in less than ten minutes.

   _____

   _____

2. After the party, he not only had a headache but also indigestion.

   _____

   _____

3. After taking some aspirin, his headache went away.

   _____

   _____

4. This year, she plans on losing twenty pounds, exercising an hour a day, and eating nutritious food.

   _____

   _____

5. I made enchiladas for the party with my grandmother's special sauce.

   _____

   _____

6. This job requires you to use several word-processing programs and that you work with spreadsheets.

   _____

   _____

7. By being computer literate, your choice of jobs is wider.

   _____

   _____

8. My thumb was cut while opening a can of soup.

   _____

   _____

9. To prepare Chinese food, he uses a cast-iron wok, a carbon-steel cleaver, and a wooden chopping block.

   _____

   _____

10. The international dinner featured appetizers from France, entrees from Italy, and the desserts were Swedish.

    _____

    _____

Part Three. Add commas, colons, dashes, apostrophes, quotation marks, and italics to the following sentences wherever they are needed. *All* the sentences need some additional punctuation; some sentences may require the addition of more than one kind of punctuation mark.

11. The following days of the week were named after Scandinavian gods and goddesses Tuesday, Wednesday, Thursday, and Friday.

12. A valet parking attendants carelessness resulted in $500 worth of damage to Eric and Ellens car.

13. Why is the womens restroom always more crowded than the mens?

14. Upon becoming prime minister of Britain in 1941 Winston Churchill said I have nothing to offer but blood, toil, tears, and sweat.

15. Nothing great was ever achieved without enthusiasm said Ralph Waldo Emerson.

16. Brevity said Dorothy Parker is the soul of lingerie.

17. The short story In Cuba I Was a German Shepherd, by Ana Mendoza, was included in the book Best New American Voices 2000.

18. That's an unusual dress she's wearing if you can call something that short a dress.

19. Encouraged by the support of her family Susan remained in college and graduated with honors.

20. Those tall leafy elm trees provide a cool shady spot for a picnic table.

Harcourt, Inc.

Answers to "A" Exercises

Exercise 1A

1. Americans invest
2. investors were
3. plans allow
4. Employees use
5. funds help
6. funds accept
7. investors had
8. they purchase
9. stockbrokers used
10. programs appear
11. Investors surf
12. They read
13. conversations focus
14. gathering gives
15. columns tell
16. investments help
17. losing is
18. investing requires

Exercise 2A

1. you are / (you) try
2. museum occupies has
3. museum contains / gallery features
4. Gallery honors contains
   (Some students may include the adjectives "Native American" because these words are part of the gallery's name. We would not consider this an error. This also applies to the galleries named in #s 11, 12, and 14.)
5. Beadwork, pottery, basketry, carvings represent
6. name was / gallery pays
7. wire enabled / gallery has
8. cowboys played / collections include

Harcourt, Inc.

9. Rodeos provided / gallery re-creates
10. Visitors view learn
11. Americans learned / Gallery commemorates
12. Junction re-creates
13. guests explore visit
14. Corral allows
15. galleries display
16. museum is / it gives

Exercise 3A

1. One is
2. Sacajawea served
3. purpose was
4. Sacajawea helped
5. Sacajawea communicated
6. knowledge enabled
7. presence assured
8. woman is
9. expedition made
10. explorers traveled
11. history is
12. Sacajawea husband moved / she died
13. she returned died
14. government issued

Exercise 4A

1. tree has been described
2. tree may provide
3. people are suffering
4. diets are lacking
5. leaves contain
6. leaves are pulverized / powder is used
7. vitamin A is preventing

8. <u>supplements</u> <u>are being given</u>
9. <u>Using</u> <u>will help</u>
10. <u>seeds</u> <u>can be used</u>
11. <u>Populations</u> <u>lack</u>
12. <u>seeds</u> <u>work</u> / <u>they</u> <u>are</u>
13. <u>infections</u> <u>have been treated</u>
14. <u>ointments</u> <u>were shown</u>
15. <u>seeds</u> <u>can be crushed</u>
16. <u>Moringas</u> <u>are found</u>
17. <u>They</u> <u>can grow</u> / <u>seed</u> <u>can become</u>
18. <u>moringas</u> <u>will play</u>

Exercise 5A

1. is
2. Are
3. costs
4. is
5. seems
6. is
7. are
8. appears
9. does
10. is
11. is
12. varies
13. Has
14. are
15. Does
16. were
17. tastes
18. Have
19. is
20. Are

Harcourt, Inc.

Exercise 6A

1. has
2. have
3. drinks
4. appears
5. loves
6. are
7. are
8. is
9. is
10. Is
11. are
12. is
13. produces
14. are
15. offer
16. come

Exercise 7A

1. is
2. was
3. spends
4. meets
5. is
6. is
7. goes
8. has
9. is
10. seems
11. Were
12. serves
13. varies
14. costs
15. Is
16. needs

Harcourt, Inc.

17. was
18. appeals
19. is

Exercise 8A

1. have
2. participates
3. has
4. Does
5. takes
6. determine
7. know
8. is
9. is
10. has
11. seems
12. makes
13. has
14. is
15. Does
16. is
17. is
18. Does
19. Is
20. is

Exercise 9A

1. World; therefore, they
2. cornfields, and
3. ovens, so
4. C
5. baking; this
6. believe, but
7. dried; they

8. ailments, and
9. Europe, but
10. item, for
11. States; however, in
12. lanterns, so
13. vegetable, yet
14. jack-o'-lantern, and

Exercise 10A

1. <u>As soon as human learned to write</u> ,
2. <u>Before paper was invented</u> ,
3. <u>while the paper was still wet.</u> C
4. <u>After the tablet dried</u> ,
5. <u>Although clay was cheap and easily available</u> ,
6. <u>because they made a kind of paper from the papyrus plant.</u> C
7. <u>until they became flat sheets.</u> C
8. <u>because they could be rolled into scrolls.</u> C
9. too, but
10. wax, and
11. tablet, he
12. 100; it
13. C
14. C
15. century, they
16. hand, and
17. day, so
18. paper; however, this
19. C

Exercise 11A

Corrections will vary. The following are possible answers.

1. Because the United States . . . population, schools need
2. English; however, it has

Harcourt, Inc.

3. language, and the teacher
4. other because they have
5. language; therefore, they do
6. English, and they will
7. languages, so it may
8. teachers because not many
9. students, and students who
10. Bangladesh. In a case like this, it is
11. ESL; in this
12. students, but the emphasis
13. long, and young
14. English; meanwhile, they
15. Because students . . . languages, they may
16. adults because their native
17. possible, so these parents
18. English, and experts

Exercise 12A

Corrections will vary. The following are possible answers.

1. Americans, they
2. Countless painters have portrayed these tribes as fearless . . .
3. C
4. It started with . . . and ended with
5. American, some Plains
6. limited because they
7. C
8. task, especially for
9. Plains through intertribal
10. horses, its way
11. changes were
12. horse but were . . .

Exercise 13A

1. us, I believe, have
2. woman, for example, whose
3. objected; however, compulsive
4. surface; in fact, there
5. high; therefore, walking
6. threat; in addition, a
7. impossible; for instance, one
8. are, nevertheless, unwilling
9. C
10. fact, after
11. illness; therefore, it
12. However, a . . . required; for instance, one
13. like, for example, clearing
14. whole, compulsive

Exercise 14A

1. New Mexico, "the . . . Age," also
2. Acoma, the . . . States, has
3. mesa, an *or* mesa, an elevated plateau, 350
4. adobe, sun-dried
5. Santa Fe, the . . . capital, has
6. San Miguel, one
7. Art, one . . . colleges, attracts
8. Opera, an
9. Taos, a . . . tourism, is
10. Sumner, a . . . reservation, recalls
11. Walk, a
12. Los Alamos, the
13. Fat Man, the
14. Caverns, one
15. motto, "The

Exercise 15A

1. (foods) that Native Americans gave to the world C
2. (Columbus,) who mistakenly thought they were related to black pepper.
3. (family,) which also includes tomatoes, eggplants, and potatoes.
4. (compound) that gives the peppers their hot taste. C
5. (Scale,) which ranges from 0 for bell peppers to 5000 for (jalapeños,) which are a common ingredient in Mexican cooking.
6. (Scoville,) who first developed a standard for measuring capsaicin's powers.
7. (Habaneros,) which are the hottest of all chiles, have
8. (ways) that seem unusual to modern cooks. C
9. (Moctezuma,) who was the last Aztec emperor, drank
10. (sauce,) which appears on restaurant tables throughout the Southwest as routinely as salt and pepper.
11. (products) that can be found in the Southwest C
12. (foods) that use a lot of chiles, . . . (restaurant) that serves Mexican, Szechuan Chinese, or East Indian food. C (Comma after "chiles" because of the introductory adverb clause.)
13. (world) where peppers play an important role in the native cuisine. C
14. (properties) that enable it to be used for purposes other than food. C
15. (ointment) that is used to treat aching muscles. C
16. (sprays) that police officers use to subdue criminals . . . capsaicin, which is a powerful irritant to the eyes and the respiratory system.
17. (Relish,)," which appeared in the January 1992 edition of the *Smithsonian* magazine.
18. (author,) who sampled habaneros as part of his research, was

Exercise 16A

1. October, 10, 1781, in Yorktown, Virginia, when
2. American, British, and

Harcourt, Inc.

3. Street, Newport, Rhode Island
4. Providence, Rhode Island, . . . museum, a planetarium, and
5. Kingman, Arizona, and Malibu, California
6. C
7. May 15, 2002.
8. January 1, 2001, and
9. Byron, Keats, or
10. Lowell, Massachusetts, was
11. American Textile History Museum, the Boott Cotton Mills Museum, and
12. 965 East Lake Avenue, Burlingame, Vermont.
13. resume, proof of legal residence, and
14. C
15. wife, three small children, and

Exercise 17A

1. She explained the lesson to me.
2. You should phone him tonight.
3. They are giving a surprise party for us.
4. We will help her plan the party.
5. I have known them for ten years.
6. He needs to see you as soon as possible.
7. me
8. she
9. We
10. me
11. us
12. he
13. us
14. her
15. We
16. them
17. us
18. her
19. me
20. her

Exercise 18A

1. I
2. ourselves
3. he
4. themselves
5. I
6. we
7. Tim and me
8. C
9. my roommate and me
10. you and me
11. We artists
12. Max and I
13. her and me
14. than he
15. children and I
16. C
17. than they
18. by themselves
19. son has (no "he")
20. than he

Exercise 19A

1. its
2. he or she registers his or her (In this and similar answers, it would also be correct to use only masculine or only feminine pronouns: he registers his; she registers hers.)
3. he or she
4. his or her
5. she needs
6. he or she
7. his
8. his or her
9. C

10. his or her
11. mileage than he.
12. to us
13. than I
14. and me
15. he or she
16. C
17. than I
18. and he
19. and me
20. her

Exercise 20A

1. its
2. my partner or me
3. whose
4. yours
5. They're . . . theirs
6. You're
7. and it's
8. who's
9. you and me
10. hers . . . it's
11. whose
12. sister-in-law and me
13. he
14. they
15. we
16. I
17. me
18. her
19. they're
20. It's . . . who's

Harcourt, Inc.

Exercise 21A

1. American Senate of the United States Hillary Rodham Clinton
2. This Aunt Sarah Portland, Oregon Pacific Northwest
3. Belgium Flemish French
4. Boston Old North Church "Paul Revere's Ride" Henry Wadsworth Longfellow
5. Another *Old Ironsides* America's War of 1812 British
6. Proctor & Gamble Tide Folger's Cover Girl
7. The *Crouching Tiger, Hidden Dragon* Chinese
8. Thanksgiving Christmas
9. California New England
10. San Francisco Los Angeles
11. My Depression
12. John Steinbeck's *The Grapes of Wrath*
13. Woody Guthrie "This Land Is Your Land" "So Long, It's Been Good to Know You"
14. I Doctor Robert Bentley Daniel Freeman Hospital
15. History American World War II
16. Peruvian Spanish Inca Chinese

Exercise 22A

1. California, buyers
2. live: it
3. dollars'
4. everyone's
5. Robert – if . . . himself – is
6. small, inexpensive
7. dishes: baked
8. said, "There . . . peace."
9. "The . . . bullet," said
10. "Brevity," said Shakespeare, "is . . . wit."
11. *Newsweek* "Oprah on Oprah," which
12. said, "I . . . are."
13. *Paradise* *The Poisonwood Bible*
14. "Tonight" *West Side Story*

15. *West Side Story Romeo and Juliet*
16. Maria's Juliet's
17. rich, my
18. winning – only . . . million – are
19. exam, the "A Worn Path" *The Collected Stories of Eudora Welty*
20. "How . . . be?" asked
21. "Everyday Use"?

Exercise 23A

Answers will vary. The following are possible revisions.

1. By the time Bob was ten, his parents were divorced.
2. a beautiful young woman wearing a Rolex watch and driving an expensive sports car.
3. while I am driving to work
4. Date trees, which are resistant to drought, were planted in the desert by farmers.
5. while she was waiting in the dentist's office
6. coffee that was hot enough to cause serious burns to a customer
7. C
8. the leftover food that was spoiled
9. After Rob played with his children, his back muscles were sore.
10. after she argues with her husband.
11 – 15:   Answers will vary.

Exercise 24A

Answers will vary. The following are possible revisions.

1. poorly prepared food, high prices, and slow service
2. to eat less, exercise more, and stop smoking
3. you get either a Hawaiian vacation or $5000
4. in both football and baseball
5. your name, your address, and your phone number
6. must have not only beauty but also poise and intelligence

Harcourt, Inc.

7. C
8. poor acting, unrealistic special effects, and a boring plot
9. graduating from college and getting a good job.
10. hearing no evil, seeing no evil, and speaking no evil

Exercise 25A

1. begun
2. built
3. drove
4. hidden
5. spent
6. worn
7. stolen
8. met
9. read
10. sent
11. fallen
12. hurt
13. kept
14. caught
15. found
16. felt
17. swore
18. written
19. swam
20. sank
21. slept
22. taken
23. ridden
24. paid
25. fed
26. chosen
27. grew
28. rose
29. laid
30. set

INDEX

Harcourt, Inc.